L. Perry Wilbur is the author of the highly successful *The Fast Track to Success* (Prentice-Hall) and nine other books. He has won two George Washington Honor Awards for writing from Freedoms Foundation at Valley Forge and is a consultant, national magazine writer, and public speaker.

PRENTICE-HALL INTERNATIONAL, INC., London
PRENTICE-HALL OF AUSTRALIA PTY. LIMITED, Sydney
PRENTICE-HALL CANADA INC., Toronto
PRENTICE-HALL OF INDIA PRIVATE LIMITED, New Delhi
PRENTICE-HALL OF JAPAN, INC., Tokyo
PRENTICE-HALL OF SOUTHEAST ASIA PTE. LTD., Singapore
WHITEHALL BOOKS LIMITED, Wellington, New Zealand
EDITORA PRENTICE-HALL DO BRASIL LTDA., Rio de Janeiro

Getting UP
When You're Down

How You Can Overcome Disillusionment to Achieve a Sense of Satisfaction in Life

L. PERRY WILBUR

A SPECTRUM BOOK

Prentice-Hall, Inc., Englewood Cliffs, New Jersey 07632

Library of Congress Cataloging in Publication Data

Wilbur, L. Perry.
    Getting up when you're down.

    "A Spectrum Book"
    Bibliography: p.
    Includes index.
    1. Success. 2. Satisfaction. I. Title.
BF637.S8W515   1983   158'.1   83-8679
ISBN 0-13-354688-8
ISBN 0-13-354670-5 (pbk.)

10 9 8 7 6 5 4 3 2 1

ISBN 0-13-354688-8

ISBN 0-13-354670-5 {PBK.}

Editorial/production supervision by Chris McMorrow
Cover design © 1983 by Jeannette Jacobs
Manufacturing buyer: Christine Johnston

This book is available at a special discount when ordered in
bulk quantities. Contact Prentice-Hall, Inc., General
Publishing Division, Special Sales, Englewood Cliffs, N.J. 07632.

For anyone and everyone who has been, is now, or ever will be *disillusioned*—in the strong assurance that both life and the world are too fascinating and interesting to ever feel disillusioned, lonely, depressed, or unhappy for long.

Contents

20

Foreword

The writing of this book was inspired by the author as a prescription for the countless number of men and women today who are coping unsuccessfully with the problem of disillusionment.

No one can deny the fact that we are currently going through a difficult period in history as evidenced by worldwide unrest, terrorist acts of violence, our increasing crime rate, the unresolved wars in the Middle East resulting in the senseless killings of human beings, the attempts to assassinate the Pope and our own President Reagan. Is it any wonder that we ask: "What is the world coming to?"

Nevertheless, it is no time for gloom and despair. To allow yourself to justify your disillusionment, to lose faith in mankind, to be pessimistic about the future is *self-defeating*. It is negative thinking.

To blame your disillusioned feelings on the fact that you have experienced major disappointments, that fate has been unkind to you, that your prayers have gone unanswered, that the world is sick, at best is a *rationalization* for your own unhappiness.

Let's face it—life has been the survival of the fittest since the beginning of time. The world has always had problems, problems, problems, but this is no reason to become despondent and disillusioned. Civilization has its imperfections, as Freud warned us. But civilization is also *self-healing.* We have profited from our past mistakes. Its comforting to know that we are solidly against war, unjustified aggression, and acts of violence.

It is far wiser and more intelligent to be optimistic than to be cynical—that things are getting better and will continue to be better despite anything and everything. Life is beautiful. You have many things to be grateful for. To use an analogy—think of your glass not as half-empty but as half-full. It's all in your attitude.

The author cautions you not to lose hope but to assume an optimistic viewpoint of yourself and the world around you.

Getting Up When You're Down teaches you how to overcome disillusionment—how to restore your enthusiasm for day-to-day living (what the French refer to as the *joie de vivre.*)

Morbid disillusionment is incompatible with happiness, serenity, and peace of mind. Too many today are using disillusionment as a cop-out for indulging in self-destructive forms of escapism, via alcohol, drug dependency, and health-dissipations.

Disillusionment, as the author points out, arises from conflicts within *yourself,* from your own irrational fears and anxieties.

There is no valid reason why you should allow disillusionment to prevent you from leading a happy, useful life.

L. Perry Wilbur is to be congratulated for writing a book that should be read by everyone. I recommend it as extremely helpful by giving *all* of us hope for healthier thinking and happier living.

Frank S. Caprio, M.D.

The Clock
Is Ticking

1

The spellbinding film *Casablanca* was on television the other night. Watching it again makes you realize how quickly the old clock on the wall is ticking by the years. *Casablanca* was a film made in 1942. Over forty years have flown by since the film first hit the screens of the nation and won the Oscar as best movie of the year.

Humphrey Bogart, who played Rick so unforgettably in the film, would be eighty-two now had he lived. Claude Rains, Peter Lorre, and Sydney Greenstreet are gone. Ingrid Bergman is gone now too. In fact, Paul Henried is the only main actor of the film who is still alive. That makes you a bit sad when watching the wonderful old movie.

All those talented actors were in their prime when *Casablanca* was being filmed. Unknown to many, nobody in the movie knew what was going to happen in the story the next day. The film was written as they went along. Three different endings for the story were done. The ending they went with was the one that seemed right and best of all.

Bogart was a standout in the movie and gave a superb performance. *Casablanca* made him a giant star and proved beyond any doubt that he could play the romantic lead and do it extremely well. Ingrid Bergman was very believable in her role, and Lorre, Greenstreet, and Henried added fine supporting roles. Claude Rains was highly effective. Everything about the film was

2

magic. It has proven over the years to be a classic. You get something new from the film each time you see it.

There is a *timeless quality* about really great motion pictures. *Casablanca* is one of them. In their minds and memories, millions of people everywhere have lived again that climactic moment at the end when Bogart, as Rick, tells Ingrid Bergman that the problems of just two human beings don't add up to much in the total scope of things.

The world around Rick and the woman he loved seemed to be crumbling. He loved her dearly, and she loved him. She had left him years earlier in Paris, standing on a platform as his train pulled out. He had thought she was leaving with him that day. And when she didn't show up, Rick had stood there in pain with a silly look on his face as his train pulled out of the station. Talk about disillusionment!

What Rick did that night, when he gave the letters of transit to Ingrid and her husband . . . and got them on the plane for Lisbon, was indeed a noble thing. It was the right thing, hard as it was to say goodbye to the woman he loved. You can readily see what an *inspiring* lift and boost to human courage this great film gave people in 1942 and the rest of the war years that followed.

It's hard to look disillusionment right in the eye. But you *can* face it and rise above it through your personal courage, faith, and inner resources. This book will try to help you.

Refer to individual chapters in this book when you feel the need, take some of the tests in the book, and try them again in six months or a year. Then compare your *new* scores with how you did the first time you took the tests. In this way, you can tell how well you have done against any feelings of disillusionment.

Life is too great an adventure to stay disillusioned for very long. Keep yourself too busy and interested in a variety of activities and all manner of projects for disillusionment to even have a *chance* to take control in your life. There is love, hope, and life in each and every day. As a first step, list the many *good* things about your life. Appreciate and be grateful for them, no matter how small they are.

Think of Rick and even toast yourself on occasion, saying out loud to yourself, "Here's looking at you, kid." You are stronger than you realize. There is power within you to draw on time and again.

Focusing on the
Here and Now

2

You may well remember the old saying that goes like this: "The only thing you can be sure of is today, so live it to the hilt. Tomorrow may never come." Some people feel guilty about actually patterning their lives on this idea. They remember the grasshopper and the ant, and feel the burden of the Puritan ethic.

However, there's a lot of common sense value behind the objective of living in the present.

Living Each Day as It Comes

When you feel disillusioned about life, or generally "down," there are sound reasons for taking and living each day *as it comes.* Some of these main reasons include the following:

1. If you think about all the things you must do in the months ahead, you can become overwhelmed and even depressed by it.
2. The worries, troubles, heartaches, problems, and series of life's little irritations add up. But by taking only what comes each day—only what life throws at you in the course of a single period, meaning today—you can handle it and cope with it more easily.
3. Thinking too much about either your past or your future wastes time and energy. You can't change the past so why not let it go?

6

Why continually dwell on something that happened months or even years ago? Let it go. This allows you to focus all your strength and attention on what you face in the present.

If it's important to live in the present, what are some ways to specifically focus on the here and now? Here are some guidelines that have proven to be helpful to others:

- Don't go to bed at night until you *know* what your major priorities and objectives are for the next day.
- *Write* out each one of your priorities for the following day and be as clear about them as possible.
- Don't list too many priorities for a single day. Keep it manageable. Three or four objectives in the course of one day may be too many, depending on their nature. But you should have a *minimum* of one priority for every day.
- Plan the next day in your mind and determine how you will go about fulfilling your objective.
- Cut out any and all things you do each day that add up to spinning your wheels. Most people waste valuable time each day. By eliminating activities that don't help you achieve your priority for each day, you will have more time and energy to devote to attaining your goal.
- A great many people seem to accomplish their major priorities and objectives for each day during the morning hours. So decide what time section of each day is best for you. Do you function or work best in the morning hours or during the afternoon? Whichever it is, reserve this time period for devoting your full attention and energies to your desired priority for that day.
- Set a limited block of time for each important priority. This will help to budget your time and enable you to accomplish more each day.

Early Morning Risers

One of the very best ways to focus more on the here and now of your life is to become an *early morning riser.* This may prove to be more difficult than it sounds if you're not used to getting up extra early. There's no question that early morning risers tend to get more done with each day. A great many of them certainly appear to be satisfied with their daily progress and achievements.

A New York author is up at his typewriter by 5:00 every morning. He claims that he gets an enormous head start on each day in this way. By 9:00, he's already put in four good hours on his current project. He also believes that he's at his very best in the early morning hours. Years earlier, he tried working late at night and discovered that his mind rebelled. He would continually doze off at his desk. But the mornings are when he's fresh and most alert. He says that switching to the morning has paid off in many ways for him.

Other Ways to Focus on the Here and Now

What else can you do in your life to focus on the here and now? Here are some additional suggestions that have worked well for many others:

1. *Get interested in some current cause or issue.* Look at the nuclear freeze movement, for example, going on all over the world at this writing. This movement is for now, today, and the present. And those who are active in it strongly believe there may not be a tomorrow, or future, for planet earth unless they act today.

2. *Reserve enough time daily to keep up with what is happening in the world.* With television news programs and a variety of magazines and newspapers available, the opportunity is there for everyone to stay well posted on the changing economy, the trouble spots around the globe, the weather, the political picture in Washington, the arts, new scientific discoveries, inventions, food and nutrition, the latest facts on physical fitness, and so on.

The other day in a supermarket, the woman who often adds up my purchases at the checkout counter told me proudly that she has *quit* reading newspapers and watching television news entirely: "I'd rather not hear all the terrible news and garbage that's going on," she said. Granted, most of the news is negative, if not depressing, but I still believe it's far better to be aware of what is happening in the world in which you live. To believe that "ignorance is bliss" is folly.

The mere fact that you stay aware of current events will

8

enable you to better focus on the here and now. Much of what happens in this world sooner or later has an effect on us. Life was not meant to be a rose garden, and each one of us must learn to take the bitter with the sweet.

3. *Wrestle with the problems you face each day.* This in itself will result in a sharper focusing on the here and now of your life. The art of coping with problems can be *acquired.* And facing plus solving (or rising above) problems will bring a deep sense of personal satisfaction to you.

4. *Master some subject or area of interest to you.* Become so knowledgeable or skillful at it that you are, in effect, an authority. Remember the famous Birdman of Alcatraz? Strauss didn't dwell on the fact that he was in prison for life. He was too busy each day, in the *here and now,* taking care of his birds, studying various bird diseases, curing the sick ones, and providing other very young ones with tender loving care. He became a true expert and authority on birds. This *mastery* of one field or subject is an excellent and long proven way to rise above disillusionment. The reason is because becoming an expert makes you a far more enthusiastic and interesting person. It is proof that you've really accomplished something with your time. Even if you never get close to the expert level, you can pick a field and certainly become a real authority on it.

Broadway and motion picture star Ann Miller made her name in the entertainment world as a super tap dancer. But not many know that a terrible accident in a St. Louis theater in 1973 nearly ended her career. Miller had just finished a number and turned to walk off-stage. Suddenly a button was pushed at the wrong time, and the boom came down and crushed her skull. Doctors didn't believe she would ever dance again. She was in the hospital two months and was unable to walk without help for two years.

What saved the talented dancer was a stiff wig like the one she wore in her Broadway stage hit "Sugar Babies."

Ann Miller didn't moan that her career and future were gone. She had written a book about her life and career called *Miller's High Life.* As soon as she was physically able, she hit the road to promote her book. "The book saved my sanity, because going on the road made me feel like I was doing something." She couldn't dance at that time and wasn't sure if she ever would again.

So Miller really focused on what she *was* able to do in the here and now and didn't let what had happened, or the future question of whether she would ever dance again, destroy her. She focused on what she *could* do in the present.

So focus on the here and now of your life. All you really have is *today*. The following poem (author unknown) was seen outside the entrance of a church in Vancouver, Canada. Keep it in mind. Better still, read it over aloud frequently or whenever you wish to zero in on the here and now of your life and get more out of each of your todays.

TODAY

Let me be aware of the treasure you are
Let me learn from you, love you, savor you,
bless you . . . before you depart
Let me not pass you by in quest of some rare
and perfect tomorrow
Let me hold you while I may . . . for it will not
always be so
One day I shall dig my fingers into the earth
Or bury my face in a pillow
Or stretch myself taut
Or raise my hands to the sky
And want, more than all the world, your return.

One Person's Life Touches So Many Others

3

No doubt you've heard the saying that all of us are pebbles in a stream or drops in the ocean. Maybe we are, but it's surprising, when you think about it, just how interrelated most of us are. What you and I do has an effect, and often an influence, on those around us. Whatever the location or walk of life, one person's life touches many others.

Close your eyes with me now and go back in time to your school or college days. See yourself once again in the classroom of your favorite teacher or professor. In looking back, can't you see how this teacher you liked and learned from touched your life? Think about how many other young lives this same teacher may have touched and influenced.

The Example of George Bailey

There was a marvelous film back in 1947 called *It's a Wonderful Life*. It starred Jimmy Stewart in what has become a classic role— the part of George Bailey. Bailey dreamed of traveling all over the world, but what he actually did was to give the money meant for his own college education to his kid brother, Harry. George also stayed in his home town and took up the fight of his father to keep a savings and loan business from being taken over by a man named Potter, the greediest and meanest man in town.

Because George Bailey stayed in town at the helm of the bank, many families were able to get out of the slum dwellings in town (owned by Potter) and to move into lovely little homes in a bright new subdivision named Bailey Park.

The whole point of George Bailey's story, as he finds out in a very convincing way, is that his life touched the lives of many others with goodness. Even as a teenager, George had saved the life of his kid brother, Harry, when the youngster fell through some thin ice and nearly drowned. Harry grew up to become a naval war hero and flying ace. He saved the lives of all those aboard a transport ship when he shot down some enemy planes. But Harry would never have grown up to save all those lives if George hadn't been there to save his brother from drowning in the icy water.

Examples from Real Life

There are, of course, many examples of this same truth from real life.

A few summers ago, I returned to the small town in Indiana where I spent my boyhood years. The experience was both sweet and painful. I walked again the paths I had known as a boy. I stood beside the home of old friends I had loved as a boy. They were gone now, and the houses they lived in seemed strange—with new names, faces, and families in them.

There was a dear woman named Mrs. Green. She and her husband had lived just half a block from my home. I remembered, as a youngster, cutting the grass and raking leaves in her large front lawn. Now the lawn looked small. The house appeared to be closed. And I knew that Mrs. Green and her husband had died years ago. Yet, somehow, they were still there. The house that had been their home still seemed to breathe and whisper the spirit of their personalities. The house had appeared to be strange at first, when I saw it after a number of years. But my thoughts of them seemed to fill their old home once again with their spirits. I could see clear and vibrant pictures of them in my mind's eye. In a real sense, they were still very much present. Then I knew that the friendship, kindness, and love we experienced in our childhood days somehow *stays* with us. In that moment, I knew how a person's life can touch the lives of others.

John O'Hara, the brilliant novelist and short story writer, scored a real point in his first big novel of the 1930s, *Appointment in Samarra*. Each one of us must one day keep our appointment in Samarra, our day with the transition from this life to the next. Before that day arrives for each of us, we have many chances to *touch the lives* of others for the better. It may be only a smile, a friendly word, or doing some little act of kindness for someone else. Whatever it is, it might come at the right time to help another along the way.

Paul Francis Webster, a talented songwriter and brilliant lyricist, has written the unforgettable lyrics for such international song hits as "Love Is a Many-Splendored Thing," "Somewhere, My Love," "The Green Leaves of Summer," "The Shadow of Your Smile," and "Secret Love." He's won three Academy Awards for his songs and has been nominated for the Oscar another fifteen times. Think about how many lives he has enriched with his songs. His songs say something and do it with meaning, grace, and quality. They will endure for a long time to come.

How about today's busy advertising copywriters? Print ads and radio-television commercials bombard us each day to buy and use certain products or services. This, too, is touching the lives of others and persuading them logically and entertainingly to buy any one of hundreds of products. Television's very popular Mrs. Olson is a good example. She's been introducing Folger's Coffee to millions of people over the years and is like a cherished friend to us by now. She has certainly touched lives. Just seeing and hearing her enthusiasm on television brightens the moment, because she is so well known.

The work of a circus performer is another example of someone who has an influence on others. Think of the thousands, if not millions, of children who benefit from a visit each year to the circus. Whether they're a high-wire team, clowns, animal stunt men, or lion tamers, circus performers touch the lives of children and adults as well. To make others laugh and to bring some joy into their lives and entertain them, if only for a few hours, is to certainly make your life and energy count in a good way.

Bing Crosby Touched Us All

How can anyone sum up the life and career of Bing Crosby? The words come hard in trying to describe what he meant to us. He made our hearts beat a little faster whenever he sang, acted, or clowned with Bob Hope, Louis Armstrong, Danny Kaye, and many others.

When asked if he had ever taken any singing lessons, Crosby recalled what happened after he returned from his first visit to a voice teacher: "Some of my friends began needling me about it, so I never went back for more lessons."

Crosby's unique voice will never really be silent in the years ahead. It's etched forever in the sound grooves of our minds and memories. Each one of us will hear him again in the music track of our inner minds. Each one of us will find that rich, melodious, and resonant bass-baritone voice of his impossible to forget. And who would want to forget it?

"White Christmas," particularly, is Bing's song forever. We'll hear it each Christmas and see him again sitting at a piano, beside a fireplace, or riding in a sleigh. No matter who performs the song or where we may hear it, we'll listen with fond memories to the man who made all of our Christmases a little whiter and brighter.

Flashback: I was just a kid living in Indiana. It was the 1940s, back when you could hear the lyrics of a song clearly and feel the richness of the melody that supported them. One day I was playing in the living room. The radio was on. Suddenly I heard a deep rich voice singing. It was wonderful. It got to me. I can still hear it now, as though it were yesterday. I lost interest in what I had been doing and just sat there listening to Bing singing "Sunday, Monday, or Always." The *way* he was singing the song thrilled me. I had loved music from an early age, and I knew that I wanted to hear more from this singer.

From that day on, I was a Bing Crosby fan. I will always be. No other singer could ever duplicate his unique style. There was only one voice like his through the years. And the moment you heard it, you knew it was Bing. He touched all our lives in a marvelous and unforgettable way.

The same is true for other fine entertainers and stars, including Judy Garland, Fred Astaire, George and Ira Gershwin, Gene Autry, Marilyn Monroe, Elvis Presley, John Wayne, Richard Rodgers, Irving Berlin, Gene Kelly, Jimmy Durante, Humphrey Bogart, Gary Cooper, Agnes Moorehead, Rosalind Russell, and many others. Millions of people the world over will never forget Henry Fonda in his last screen role in *On Golden Pond.* Fonda's honesty, decency, and character came across on the screen as well as in person.

Many still remember their commanding officer from their military days. I well remember the man who was completely dedicated to training our navy boot camp company to be the best possible. And he did it with discipline. He taught us in twelve weeks to respect discipline and to use it in our daily lives. Some of the men griped about his yelling at them during the early days of boot camp training, and they also complained about the endless rules we had to follow. But all of us came out of boot camp far better men for the experience. And most of us said on graduation from our basic training that if we had to fight someday, we would want to follow a tough and capable leader like our company commander.

You can think of many people in your life who showed you a bit of light along the way, encouraged or inspired you, taught you one or more things that will stay with you for life, eased your burden, cheered you when you may have needed it most, helped you find the right kind of job or career for you, defended you in time of trouble, stood by you when you needed somebody on your team, and so on.

Parents have a deep and lasting influence. I often think of how much I owe my parents for all they've done for me through the years. They taught me the true meaning of success, the enduring values of life, and the tremendously important truth that you have to make your own happiness. My grandmother also touched my life in many inspiring ways.

Negative Examples

There are, of course, negative examples of this same idea. Lots of people have touched the lives of others in a negative, or even terrible, way.

Directly or indirectly, some fifty million people lost their lives in World War II because of Adolf Hitler. If he had never been born, those millions who went to their graves because of him could have lived out their lives and had the same chance many of us today take for granted.

The cruelty, misery, genocide, starvation, pain, hardships, chaotic conditions, loss of basic freedoms, and whole catalog of horrors caused by the Third Reich are well known by now. It's one thing to read about such unbelievable cruelty and lack of humanity, but something else to have lived through it . . . or endured it until death set you free.

Hitler led them, but the Nazi officers, Gestapo, death camp commanders, agents, and soldiers, as well as others, share the blame.

More modern negative examples include any and all rip-off artists, swindlers, tricksters, crooked politicians, and all who lie awake at night thinking of new schemes to cheat and profit from their fellow man.

How You Can Touch the Lives of Others with Goodness

Here are some guidelines and proven ways by which you can touch the lives of others for good:

1. *Show you care.* When those around you are upset, concerned, disillusioned, heartbroken, disappointed, worried, angry, anxious, sad, or whatever, let them know that you care about them and want to help. Just knowing that another human being really cares is comforting.

2. *Encourage others whenever you can.* A word of encouragement can do much to help others believe in themselves more, try a new field of endeavor, keep going on, explore or develop their talents, and generally get more out of their lives.

3. *Be an inspiring person.* Whatever your work is and wherever you live, there are people in your life who look up to you and can learn from your example. By trying to be an inspiring person, you thus have a direct opportunity to influence the goals and lives of others for the better.

4. *Be a consistently loyal friend.* When lucky individuals win one of the various million dollar lotteries or come into other fortunate circumstances, they're always amazed that old friends (they haven't seen in some time) and sudden new ones (they didn't know they had) come out of the woodwork. By being a consistently loyal friend, you will have a real and lasting influence on those in your life. Like a grocer friend of mine said one day, "As you grow older, you can count your *real* friends on half the fingers of one hand."

5. *Make an important contribution to society or humanity.* Millions of lives have been touched and enriched by the likes of such contributors as Winston Churchill, Helen Keller, Albert Einstein, Thomas Edison, Bob Hope, Katharine Hepburn, Ronald Reagan, Hubert Humphrey, Dwight D. Eisenhower, Harry S. Truman, George M. Cohan, Kate Smith, and many others. The idea of making a lasting contribution can have the effect of touching the lives of an enormous number of people everywhere for good.

I often think of a quote I came across by Cecil B. DeMille, the legendary film producer. This was a statement DeMille made not long before his death. When a friend asked how he was, DeMille, who knew he didn't have long to live, replied that he felt it was about time to be moving on and that what he was thinking about was "another film, another life, and maybe even another world." I like to think that he's continuing to touch the lives of others . . . continuing to make a contribution in the life beyond.

Whoever you are and whatever the circumstances and routine of your life may be, try not to miss the chance to touch someone else's life for the better each and every day. It may be just a smile or a cheerful word, but you will leave the other person a little warmer and a bit more enriched. In doing so, you will live a more noble life: "For if you have done it unto the least of these, my brethren, you have done it unto me."

The Frantic Search
for Escape
from Reality

With the dawn of each new day, millions wonder how they can escape from reality during the hours ahead. Some take their escape via the bottle and get mind-staggering drunk. Others go the drug routine or lose themselves in sleep. All of them have one sad objective in common—a desire to escape from the real world.

On June 26, 1982, in Chicago, Ellen Chow and Edmund DeBock climbed the fire escape to the top floor of the six-story Y.M.C.A. building. They held hands for a moment and then jumped. Ellen was killed, and Edmund was critically injured. Two of the couple's young friends said that Ellen and Edmund told them they were going to kill themselves, calling it "their way of finding a better world." Karen Geisheker and Michael Urban, friends of the couple, tried to talk them into coming down. So did a guard. "They had been talking about killing themselves for months," said Urban. Ellen had tried to slit her wrists the winter before. Her last words before climbing to the top of the building were, "Tell my family I love them."

The Tragic Death
of William Holden

I was quite a fan of the late actor William Holden. Like many others, I saw all of his films and admired his acting ability a great deal. He was one of the finest actors of the century.

20

From reports of his death, William Holden would be alive today if he hadn't been drinking in his apartment alone for days. In that condition, he fell and cut his head on the sharp edge of a table. Had he not been drinking, the accident would not have happened. He reportedly drank too much at various times and, for whatever reasons, wished to escape from reality.

I remember Holden as the young army officer he played in the *Dear Ruth* series of films during the 1940s. But the 1950s brought his best movie years, starting with *Sunset Boulevard* in 1950 and continuing with such marvelous blockbuster films as *Stalag 17* (for which he won the Oscar for best actor), *Sabrina, Love Is a Many-Splendored Thing, The Country Girl,* and others.

The Rising Suicide Rate

Some persons flee from reality by taking their own lives. While women reportedly lead in attempted suicides, four times as many American men kill themselves as do women. Are the large cities to blame? Authorities state that the suicide rate is highest in big cities and lowest in country areas. Perhaps the pace is too fast or frustrating for many city dwellers.

Even gloomy weather can lead to more suicides. Many people just can't help being influenced by the weather. I once knew a college student who couldn't study at all whenever it rained. Try as she did, she was no good at the books as long as it was raining outside. Some people hear or read a bad weather report and immediately feel worse.

The sight of the magnificent Golden Gate bridge in San Francisco is quite majestic, but this is the spot where hundreds of people have chosen to exit from this world. Because of this dramatic way to "go out in style," San Francisco has almost *five times* the suicide rate of New York. New York has bridges too, of course, but none of them can quite measure up to the Golden Gate.

How many succeed in escaping reality by killing themselves? In the United States, out of more than one hundred thousand who try suicide each year, close to twenty thousand succeed. And these figures are increasing.

According to *Statistical Abstract,* the state of Nevada had the highest rate of suicide in a recent year. The rate there was 26.7

21

per one hundred thousand population. Alaska ran a close second with a 19.4 percent rate. Hungary, at this writing, is the world capital for suicide with a whopping 40.7 per one hundred thousand population.

While suicide may look like a way out, an escape from grim reality, a great many people believe that anyone who takes his or her life will have to bear the consequences for such an act. Most Christian believers throughout the world think that the worst thing a person can do is to snuff out his or her own life. "Life is God's greatest gift," they say. Those also who profess belief in reincarnation, and their number is now reported to be half the people in the world, claim that "suicide is no escape at all. It simply delays and holds back a soul's growth and progress. Whoever takes his life will have to come back to earth and face the same situation, or problem, once again. So there really is no escape."

Escape via Romance Novels

Millions of women readers escape every day, or several times a week, in the pages of historical and contemporary romance novels. The sales of these novels have skyrocketed during the last few years, and the demand for romantic fiction shows no sign of slowing down at this writing.

Part of the reason for the wide popularity of romance novels is that many single and married women readers desire more romance in their lives.

The chance to enter a new and thrilling world of romance, if only vicariously through the experience of the lead character, is too appealing to resist. So an enormous number of women readers (and some men as well) forget their problems for awhile and live the life of another woman, who is soon involved in an exciting romance, often in a glamorous or intriguing locale.

British author Barbara Cartland has helped many millions of women in numerous countries to escape their personal problems and worries. As the acknowledged queen of romantic fiction, Barbara Cartland published an amazing twenty-four different romance novels in a recent year. Over seven million copies of her books were shipped to American bookstores alone during that one year. A report in *Publishers Weekly,* the major trade publication for the book field, stated that total sales of her novels have passed the $100 million mark.

Escaping by Watching Television

Millions of others choose the one-eyed monster as their way to escape reality. Many of these individuals have become television addicts over the years. They simply can't get through the day or night without sitting in front of their television sets for hours at a time . . . or even all day long. They've become television addicts, much like the viewers described by the memorable news anchor man in the film *Network*. The tube does all their thinking and eventually suspends their minds. They stumble away from the tube almost hypnotized by the effects of too much viewing.

Families used to be very close. Everyone did things together. They prayed and played together. They talked, shared, and actually grew together. Today the lack of communication in the average family is both obvious and tragic. As the late cartoonist Al Capp said so well, "Today's kids are raised by the television set."

With cable television now available in most large cities, viewers have an incredible number of channels to choose from, which is sure to mean that more people than ever before will be spending huge chunks of their lives glued in front of the tube. After all, it is easier to snap on the tube than to talk out one's problems. It's more tempting to enter another land, or follow a series, or keep up with a soap opera via the tube than to pursue an active hobby or interest, get together with others, read something informative and stimulating, have a family discussion, take part in some local or civic cause, and generally be a *doer* yourself.

A man in Tennessee stated his feeling for television in this way: "I grew up in a home where there was no television, and my wife and I do not have one in our home. Our present opinion is not to ever have one. I've taken up the hobby of designing and building furniture and have built a bedroom suite for my wife and one for each of our two daughters."

This is not to say that it's *all* thumbs down for television. There are some fine news programs offered each week, and public television has done much to raise viewing standards. But when television becomes a crutch and a means of escaping reality for too

23

long a time period, it can soak up your mind and life like a sponge, leaving you little time for other worthwhile interests and pursuits. It's like the old, but still very true, cliché—"moderation in everything."

The Escape of James Dean and Elvis Presley

Many believe to this day that actor James Dean's death on a California highway, on September 30, 1955, was the result of his frantic effort to escape. Dean's form of escape was to race his sports car at high speeds, almost tempting fate to do what it would with him.

Elvis Presley was unhappy after the breakup of his marriage. Not being able to go out by daylight and live his life in a normal way no doubt increased his desire to escape his prison-like existence. In the last years of his life, he felt the need to escape more and more from his unhappiness.

But America and the world can only admire the late actress Ingrid Bergman. Instead of ducking out on reality, she bravely faced it head on. With all the fame she won, Ingrid refused to dwell on the past. She accepted the full responsibility for what she did in 1949, when she left the security of a Hollywood career and marriage to marry Italian producer, Roberto Rossellini. She faced the reality of what she had done when she returned to Hollywood in 1956. And she won over the people again.

Above all, in 1973 Ingrid Bergman faced the fact that she had cancer and did the best she could. In one of her last statements, her courage was evident: "Time is shortening. I've accepted it, and I will make the most of what's left of my life. Our days are counted, but you can't worry about them."

How to Face Reality in Your Life

Here are some useful guidelines that will help you face reality in your daily life:

- *Try to learn to take what life throws at you.* Everyone has some problems and troubles. Nobody is completely immune. Even Christ said that life was no rose garden . . . no bed of roses.

- *Don't overprotect yourself.* Be willing to take chances and to risk possible failure. Every day is a gamble in a number of ways.

- *Know and depend on the truth that there is a vast reservoir of power within you* on which you can draw time and again to face what you must each day . . . or at difficult times in your life.

- *Remember that everyone is disillusioned at various times in his or her life.* It's how you react to it and what you do about it that is important. The strength and resources to rise above a sense of disillusionment is inside you. You are a much stronger person than you realize. Help someone less fortunate than you are, read the Bible or other inspiring material, use one or more positive slogans, and focus your attention on the many good things about your life. When you really think about it, *reality* is the best thing we've got going here on earth, whatever the problems, troubles, heartaches, and irritations connected with it may be.

- *Believe and stay confident that you were born to be a champion.* You really were. Know that you can and will cope with anything.

- *Realize that running away from reality never solves anything.* The problem is usually still there when you get back. Meet it head on and conquer it.

- *Strive to learn to like, appreciate, and place greater value on reality,* for it is life.

You Have to Make Your Own Happiness

5

In the unforgettable film, *Love Is a Many-Splendored Thing,* William Holden and Jennifer Jones, as the characters in the story, are together at the top of their favorite hill overlooking Hong Kong. A beautiful butterfly suddenly lands on Holden's shoulder, and Jennifer tells him to stand still and not to move because it's a good omen.

Little did either of them know at that moment how short a time they had, in the story, to be happy together. People in both of their lives were trying to keep them apart. And, as things turned out, the character played by Holden was soon killed in Korea while working as a war correspondent.

But they had been happy together, if only for a short time. They made their own happiness by not letting gossip, traditional customs, or bossy friends come between them. Holden reminds her how lucky and blessed they have been to find *true* love in, and with, each other.

That film, released in 1955, still gets to me each time I see it. It is a beautiful love story, but there is more. There are a number of timeless truths expressed in the film. I always get caught up in the story of this doctor and journalist, and the film makes it very clear, in a vividly dramatic way, that you have to *make* your own happiness. You can't expect it to just arrive on your doorstep like the daily paper. You've got to get out there and make your own happiness . . . for as short or long a time as it lasts.

A Class in School on Happiness

It has long been my belief that the schools and colleges of our land, and others too, should offer regular class instruction on happiness. Many people, both young and older, assume that happiness either comes to a person or does not. Millions spend their entire lives with the false belief that some people are meant to be happy and others are not . . . that there's nothing they can do by themselves to become happier individuals.

A regular class dealing with happiness could investigate *all aspects* of it, discuss all definitions of it, explore why some people find happiness and others don't, and show students in the course how to increase their chances for happiness in their lives. Such a course, if well planned and taught by the right person, might well prove to be more important in the long run than the other traditional, strictly academic subjects. Can't you see such a course listed in the college catalog—maybe as Happiness 101 and 102? No doubt it would fill up faster than any other course of study.

Happiness Is Definitions

Just as success does, happiness clearly means different things to various people. To show you the wide variety of definitions of happiness, consider the following frequently voiced statements. And note that some are serious, while others are meant to be funny, frivolous, or silly.

- Happiness is catching a rising stock on its way up.
- Happiness is a soft puppy dog.
- Happiness is someone to share your life with.
- Happiness is warm feet on a cold winter night.
- Happiness is going back to Rome and remembering the first coin you threw in the fountain.
- Happiness is a bowl of Cheerios and a ripe banana.

- Happiness is remembering *any* scene from *Casablanca,* but especially when Bogart tells Ingrid Bergman, "Here's looking at you, kid."
- Happiness is a good book to read and a comfortable chair.
- Happiness is the magic of Christmastime in the city.
- Happiness is shrimp gumbo.
- Happiness is knowing where you parked your car in a crowded lot.
- Happiness is staying out of jail.
- Happiness is waking up each morning to a fresh new day.
- Happiness is the memory of a friend like E.T.
- Happiness is being with loved ones.
- Happiness is a peanut butter and jelly sandwich.
- Happiness is the colorful sights and sounds of today's modern and busy world.
- Happiness is a winning hand and knowing how to play it.
- Happiness is a Ted Williams baseball card.
- Happiness is a root beer float.
- Happiness is an orchestra seat at a Neil Simon play.
- Happiness is losing yourself in an engrossing novel.
- Happiness is a Via Rail Canada ticket from Vancouver to Montreal.
- Happiness is a weight scale that is broken.
- Happiness is a hot bath and clean underwear.
- Happiness is doing something to brighten the lives of others.

How to Make Your Own Happiness

The following guidelines have proven to be definite *steps to more happiness* for a great many people. Put them into action in your life, and I think you'll be pleased with the results:

1. *Always have pleasant or interesting things to look forward to.* This will keep happy expectations in your life. Watch your local newspaper for announcements of forthcoming events and attractions, and then see that your schedule includes a number of them.

2. *Bring happiness into the lives of others.* Then some of that happiness is bound to rub off on you.

I well remember Miller Uline, a fine man who lived most of his life in Nappanee, Indiana. He went out of his way to help my family find and get the right house when we moved to the small town in the early 1940s. He introduced us to everyone in town and did everything in his power to see that we were happy in our new surroundings. He and his wife remained good friends over the years.

My mother has brought a great deal of happiness to others. I'll never forget the wonderful meals and cakes she prepared over the years for sick friends and others who were unable to leave their homes. She also personally visited them. She has done so many kind and loving things for her many friends, neighbors, her own mother, husband, relatives, and every member of her family that she well deserves the compliment often paid to her that "she is a person who *lives* her faith all week long."

3. *Fall in love with learning.* There are so many fascinating things to discover and learn that this step alone can bring you far more happiness. Knowledge is power, and it is also increased happiness, for learning can be a joy in itself.

A group of older Americans attended a special summer session at a New England college last year. Interviewed about their time back on the campus, they said that they were having a marvelous experience going to classes again and learning new information about the subject areas of personal interest to them. The world is really filled with all types of fascinating things to learn, explore, and discuss with others.

4. *Keep the following statement in mind, as the months and years tick away: "Life isn't much without a family."* If you have a family, then you'll understand what I mean. It's true that single life has advantages, and it's nice when one is young, but it can become very lonely as you grow older.

Based on research I've done over the past five years, I'm absolutely convinced that marriage is going to make a terrific comeback in the years ahead. Getting married is a risk, of course, but the chance to have a family of your own is usually well worth it.

5. *Find the area of the country (or the world) you like and go there if possible.* Several students I knew years ago in graduate school at Emory University had dreamed of moving to Oregon for some time. After spending a summer out there, they came back to graduate school (for the last year), completely determined to go to

31

Oregon once they had their advanced degrees. The last I heard from them, they were living in several different cities in Oregon, were married with growing families, and were *happier* than ever before in their lives. As one of them wrote to me in a letter, "There's no other place for me to live but here in the great Northwest, better known as God's country."

6. *If tragedy or sorrow comes into your life, one of the most helpful ways to cope with it is to throw yourself into your work, career, or interest.* Keep yourself so busy that you have little, if any, time to dwell on what has happened.

A few years after his stupendous success in *Gone With the Wind,* actor Clark Gable's happiness dissolved in a terrible tragedy that left the popular star heartbroken and half out of his mind with grief. Gable had married actress Carole Lombard, and the two had been very happy for a few short years. She had been with Gable at the Atlanta premiere of *Gone With the Wind* and had been proud of him. The two were deeply in love.

Then, in January 1942, while returning from a war bond selling tour shortly after Pearl Harbor, Carole Lombard's plane crashed in the mountains near Las Vegas. Everyone aboard the plane was killed. Half crazed with grief, Gable insisted on keeping Carole's room just as she had left it. Ironically, at the time of the tragic accident, Gable was acting in a film called, *Somewhere I'll Find You.*

After losing Carole, Gable changed. He wanted to work *harder* than ever before. He wanted things to be tough. He joined the Army Air Corps as a private at age forty-one. Maybe the actor thought that a rough period of time in the service during a war would help him to get over his deep sorrow.

Entering the service in 1942, Gable made it clear that he didn't expect or want any soft movie star type of duty. As he put it: "I don't want to make speeches. I don't want to sell bonds, I don't want to entertain. I just want to be a machine gunner on a bomber and be sent where the going is tough."

Gable somehow found the courage to go on in his new life in the service. He came out a major and got his old job back at M-G-M Studios. He had proven himself by attaining his rank the hard way. Hollywood and the entire nation respected him for it.

A pilot who had known Gable at an American bomber base

in England summed up for a reporter how he felt about having a movie star on his fighting team: "Clark came here to do a good job and he did it. He always was a good soldier, never imposed his popularity and took the bad with the good without complaining. He went on some tough missions with us and proved himself a great guy."

Another memorable example is the case of novelist Victor Hugo. Hugo's favorite brother went insane at his wedding. From that day on, the sick brother had to be confined to a sanitarium. Hugo's favorite daughter, his oldest, drowned in the Seine River and was considered a possible suicide. Tragedy after tragedy stalked this magnificent man of the written word. Hugo outlived both his sons. His younger daughter went mad after eloping with a British army officer. She spent the next fifty years in a madhouse.

Despite the incredible tragedies in his life, Victor Hugo *made his own happiness.* He did it in and through his writing. He became the wonder of France during his adult life. The author of great immortal novels like *Les Miserables,* he also wrote very popular plays, razor-sharp criticisms, and excellent lyric-epic poetry. He stayed amazingly productive, even in the face of so many mind-shattering tragedies. He, too, is an excellent example of the truth that you have to *make* your own happiness.

Note: Another book of mine may be of *special* help to you as you seek to make your own happiness. This book was written with a world-famous doctor and is called *How to Enjoy Yourself: The Antidote Book to Unhappiness and Depression.* The book gives hundreds of ideas to make your life more fun, meaningful, and enjoyable every day of the year. It is published by Prentice-Hall, Englewood Cliffs, New Jersey 07632.

Live for Life's Lovely Intangibles

There are many people around the globe who frequently wonder why they find themselves in a disillusioned and depressed mental state. Such unhappy feelings come to most of us at times. And when they do, one of the best steps you can take is to get your head right by focusing your mind on beautiful things, such as life's lovely *intangibles.*

The Bible itself gives specific directions along these lines: "Whatsoever thoughts are beautiful, true, holy, just, and honorable—think on these things." People everywhere need to substitute their nightmares of black and pessimistic thoughts with cleansing, uplifting, and spiritual thinking.

Think of yourself as a house, which has been locked up for the long winter months. All the windows have been boarded up for four or five months. Then, with the first signs of a new spring, someone comes along and opens up all the windows. The fresh clean air rushes into the house, into every dusty corner, and drives out the stale air.

In a very real sense, that is exactly what the act of concentrating on beautiful thoughts, on life's lovely intangibles, can do for you. The clean, fresh air of *right* thinking works like a purifier. A new spring season literally takes up residence in your mind. Your thoughts become beautiful, true, honorable, and inspiring. It's then that you know in both your heart and mind that you're free again.

I want to suggest five specific, beautiful thoughts to you. They have meant a great deal to me over the years. I've tried to give them a dwelling place in my daily life. I've thought about them so often over the years that they seem like old friends to me today. These five never-failing friends are goodness, beauty, honor, truth, and love.

Some have referred to these five friends of mine as intangibles. Many would probably agree that they are some of the intangibles of life. But I want to highlight another word before intangibles—"lovely." I see nothing wrong with thinking of my five friends as lovely intangibles. For in reality, that is what they truly are.

In the unforgettable film classic of 1947, *Miracle on 34th Street,* John Payne and Maureen O'Hara have a bit of a squabble. Payne has just quit his job (as the character he plays) with a New York law firm to defend his friend and client Kris Kringle on a full-time basis. A New York court is trying to get Kringle committed.

Doris (Maureen O'Hara) is angry because Payne has thrown away his job because of his idealistic beliefs. Payne answers that the best thing about law is keeping people from being walked on and pushed around.

Growing more angry, Doris runs down the catalog of intangibles, saying that Payne is impractical. Payne then tells her that the ideals in life are what make it worth living. He clearly reveals to her that he means what he says—and that ideals mean a lot to him.

How right he was! Life's lovely intangibles add a richness beyond the price of gold and silver. They add depth, substance, and quality to life on this spinning speck of the cosmos. They make life well worth the living.

Take goodness as one intangible. Children at Christmastime are warned and advised to be good . . . "not to pout because Santa will soon be coming to town." But goodness is really its *own reward.* God made us all good. Everything he made was and is basically good. It is man who has allowed distortions, corruption, and evil into his life here on earth.

The example of the good Samaritan comes to mind. Not for a moment did the Samaritan think about *what he might get* in return for helping the man in distress. Instead, the Samaritan was a good man and did the right thing because he wanted to. It was his nature to be good, and goodness was the result.

Beauty

Beauty is another lovely intangible. To seek the beautiful in life is to live on all of your cylinders. Dutch painter Vincent van Gogh saw and captured the incredible beauty of sunlight on a field of flowers . . . and also in the face of a peasant. The beautiful smile of the Mona Lisa has conquered the hearts of millions.

Beauty is really everywhere, if you stay alert for it. It rises with every dawn and waves through sunsets; it leaves its calling card in every rainbow; it's there in the white blanket of snow that covers the land in the middle of winter; it silhouettes the sky as a flock of birds wings its way homeward; it's there looking up from the eyes of a small baby, in the melodic strain of a symphony orchestra, the precision of a ballet, or the thousands of twinkling stars in the late night sky.

Honor

What about honor? It used to be far more valuable than gold to a great many people. The lust for money, power, and position has dimmed the luster of honor. But each person must live with his or her conscience. Shakespeare said it well: "To thine own self be true."

In a difficult period of her life, when Scarlett O'Hara thought she wanted to run away with Ashley Wilkes, he rejected her. He said that he was a coward and wouldn't do it, and couldn't leave his wife and child. Ashley then reminded Scarlett that there was something to keep them there at Tara. Scarlett said that nothing was holding her there, and Wilkes replied, "Nothing but honor."

Truth

Men and women have died for the truth, fought for it, pledged their lives and fortunes to it, and sought it through the centuries. Many have not always understood it when they found it. The Bible is

God's book of truth. Andrew Jackson's last words reaffirmed his belief in the good book: "The Bible is true."

French novelist Emile Zola staked his life, career, and reputation on his belief in the truth of the innocence of Alfred Dreyfus, a wrongly imprisoned man who had been sentenced to life on Devil's Island.

Zola's letter, "I Accuse," attacked the corruption of the French army of that day and called for a new investigation of the Dreyfus case. The letter cast seeds of doubt and eventually led to the freedom of a framed and falsely convicted man.

Zola's great battle cry, which sustained him all through his life and especially through a number of trying times, consisted of these memorable words: "Truth is on the march!"

Love

"Now abideth faith, hope, and love. But the greatest of these is love." He or she who has loved and loves now knows God. For God is love. Perhaps the clearest and most wondrous example of love in action is God's love for each of us. His love was so great that He sent his own son to die for us, to take the sting of death away so that you and I might be redeemed. What greater love could He show?

So these are life's lovely intangibles. I can assure you that they are worth knowing. They will give you hope when the world seems to come on too strong. In the still of the night, they will speak to your heart and spirit and urge you to believe in them . . . only believe. Nourish them in your mind and life, and they will become your loyal friends.

Wherever you go in life, take the lovely intangibles along with you. They'll uplift you when many other ornaments of life deceive and fail you. They are life's *real riches*. They last. To know them is to know God. To live with them is to live with God. Goodness, beauty, honor, truth, and love. They can and will help you to rise above disillusionment and overcome it completely. Cherish them as life's lovely intangibles. They will be here long after you and I are gone.

Tune Up
Your Wonderful
Imagination

7

One of the most *powerful* ways to overcome a sense of disillusionment in your life is to dust off your marvelous imagination, tune it
up, and start using it every day.

A Self-Scoring Test on Your Imagination

To show you how rusty, fair, or possibly strong and healthy your
imagination currently is, answer the following questions as best you
can, then refer to the directions on scoring your answers.

		YES	NO
1.	Do you occasionally find yourself think-ing of some *new* business or service you believe would be a good one?	____	____
2.	Do you sometimes get ideas for a new product, song, short story, motion pic-ture, greeting card, game, novel, poem, play, toy, or what have you?	____	____
3.	Do you think that imagination is more important than talent?	____	____

	YES	NO
4. Do you sometimes wake up in the middle of the night to write down some notes or an idea?	____	____
5. Do you enjoy reading a variety of material a great deal?	____	____
6. Have you created anything original in the last six months?	____	____
7. Have you achieved any of your goals in life because of your imagination?	____	____
8. Do you think the invention of the paper clip was a terrific idea?	____	____
9. Do you believe your imagination can produce ideas for you on a regular basis?	____	____
10. Does the thought of doing some creative work every day excite you?	____	____

How to Score Your Test Answers

Score ten points for every YES answer and zero for each NO answer. Then add your total and place your score in this blank: _____

TEST SCORING TABLE

Score	Evaluation
90 to 100	Great! This high score means that you are a very imaginative person. Such imagination may well lead you to high levels of success and prosperity. Continue to develop even more imagination.
80 to 90	This is a good level of imagination and enough to make your life and work more interesting. You should, however, raise this level of imagination higher.
70 to 80	This shows only a fair amount of imagination. You are probably somewhat limited for imaginative projects and work unless you're able to increase this current degree.

Score	Evaluation
60 to 70	Based on this score, you are lacking in imagination. Strive to develop more imagination, and get it working for you.
50 to 60	You have little or no imagination. Start at once to develop more.

The Importance of Imagination

More and better use of imagination can help individuals and companies to prosper, grow, and be more successful. Here are just a few of the ways in which imagination has proven to be invaluable to people and businesses-industries alike:

1. *Insurance Companies.* A recent full-page newspaper ad showed how New York Life used its imagination to apply its insurance product to the appeal of starting an IRA (individual retirement account). The headline of the ad read as follows: "Everyone's after your IRA dollars. Here's how to keep from being pulled in the wrong direction." One section of the body copy of the ad also had this heading: "Our IRA will last as long as you do, too."

2. *Soft Drink Industry.* Seven-up really got the other leading name colas uptight with the simple but imaginative idea of "no caffeine." Seven-up ads proclaimed "Seven-up . . . crisp and clean . . . no caffeine . . . feelin' Seven-up."

A Seven-up television commercial showed Tug McGraw, relief pitcher for the Philadelphia Phillies, pushing away cans of other drinks including Coke, Dr. Pepper, Pepsi, Mountain Dew, and Sunkist orange soda. As McGraw pushes the others away, he says, as he reaches for Seven-up, "I'm taking no caffeine."

3. *Large City Mall Promotion.* Malls have used imagination to draw customers to their complexes of stores. Some of their lures have included the following:

- A couple actually being married in the center of the mall
- Rock-and-roll concerts
- Puppet shows
- Pony rides (to get families to the mall)
- Magicians

- Fashion shows—A well-known Chicago store put on a little girl fashion show in which all the small girls modeled clothes and wore Little Orphan Annie red wigs. It was a big success and drew a large crowd.

4. *100th Anniversary of a Town.* When a town or city celebrates its 100th anniversary, it wants the best attractions and events it can present. And that calls for *imagination.* To help celebrate its centennial, the small town of Nappanee, Indiana came up with a winner—a rocking chair contest. Whoever rocked the longest received a $250 first prize.

The idea isn't all that new, of course, and has been used by other promoters for their causes or businesses. But when I watched the one in Nappanee, Indiana, it was a first for me. It was a great success for the town. Some rocking chair contests have offered higher cash prizes, but the $250 in a small Indiana town certainly brought out plenty of eager contestants.

On the first day of the contest in Nappanee, a Friday, fifty-one young people and older adults sat down in their rocking chairs and started to rock. Each contestant was sponsored by a local business firm. All who entered came well prepared for a long siege of rocking.

Contestants brought umbrellas, newspapers, books, drinking water, sewing material, flashlights, food, and all manner of things with which to pass the time while rocking.

All of the fifty-one rockers were enthusiastic when they started. The rules required that each of their rocking chairs had to be in *continuous* rocking movement, and contestants were allowed only a seven minute bathroom-rest break each hour. The rocking continued straight through the nights, after each day of full-time rocking.

Two days after the clever promotion began, the number of contestants had dropped to thirteen. In two and one-half days, from Friday to Sunday night, thirty-eight of the original fifty-one rockers had quit.

On Monday afternoon, three days after the contest got underway, there were only five rockers left. These five brave souls had survived sixty-nine hours of rocking and were still at it. The five rockers left were all women.

A local teenage girl won the contest spectacle. After receiving the $250 first prize, she rose up from the rocker and tried to take a few steps. She couldn't walk and was stumbling, so several of her school friends picked her up and carried her to a waiting car that took her home. A large sign was later placed across the front porch of her home, declaring her to be the winner. She had rocked until 9:30 Tuesday morning—almost four days and nights.

5. *Housewives.* Busy housewives of today use imagination every day to keep their families happy and their homes running smoothly. Consider the following, as just a few of the many ways they use imagination:

- Imaginative meals
- Ideas for things the kids can do
- *Ingenious* ways to stretch the family budget
- Referee and problem solver
- Recreational director
- Getting the kids to start their homework
- Ego smoother
- Interior decorator
- Vacation organizer

6. *Teachers.* It almost goes without saying that a good teacher needs imagination to gain and hold the attention of students. This is especially true in today's modern classroom. Imagination helps a teacher explain to students:

- Why they need to study certain subjects
- The relationships of ideas, truths, and principles
- The challenges, opportunities, and rewards of learning
- The lessons of the past and the hopes for the future
- The examples and contributions of others

7. *Secretaries.* Some imaginative secretaries prove to be worth their weight in gold in the ways they help their bosses. Here are just a few:

- Ideas to save time for their boss and thus prevent backtracking
- Imaginative ways to coordinate work of their departments or groups plus others as well

- Suggestions for improvement in office routine
- Suggestions for increasing productivity
- Pinch-hitting for the boss when he or she is out of town
- Solving all manner of business or office problems

How to Tune and Sharpen
Your Imagination

The rest of this chapter offers suggestions and pointers on how you can develop your imagination and keep it in tune. The directions that follow are based on my many years of experience, research, and direct interviews with a number of highly imaginative people from different fields and walks of life. Some exercises for sharpening your imagination are also included on the last page of this chapter. Here are the suggestions for improving your imagination:

1. Decide in what area or field you wish to apply your imagination. In other words, what is it you want to use your imagination on? Is it a business situation, a personal or family problem, a new invention, how to make your time count more, an audio-visual script, a training film, a print ad or radio-television commercial, interior decorating in your home, or what?

2. Start an ongoing program meant to increase the *intensity* and *keenness* of your imagination. In the words of Brooks Atkinson, the famous drama critic, "Every person can achieve a great deal . . . according to the burning intensity of his will and the keenness of his imagination." Your program to sharpen your imagination should consist of the following steps:

- Begin at once to read magazine articles and books on imagination. Don't overlook a number of books you can buy, or get from your library, that deal with creativity as it relates to imagination. A fine variety of magazine articles on imagination can be found by checking the *Reader's Guide to Periodic Literature* in your library.

- Buy yourself a fairly large three-ring notebook, filled with paper, and keep it handy, either at home or in your office . . . or place where you work (if possible). Whenever your time allows, write down in this notebook anything and everything you believe is helpful, informative, or worth remembering dealing with imagination. I assure you that this step alone will *greatly increase* your knowledge and understanding of imagination. I started such a notebook many years ago, and it has grown very thick by now. It has proven to be a gold mine of information and inspiration on imagination. I consider it to be much more valuable than a university degree or Ph.D. in the subject.

• Study the lives of individuals who were, or are, highly imaginative. Find out what made them that way. Were they *born* with four-star imaginations, or did they develop this magic commodity? Here are just a few examples of those whose lives and careers you might wish to investigate: Thomas Edison (he kept diaries you can look over), Walt Disney, Harry Houdini, Conrad Hilton, dancer-singer-actress Ann Miller, Bette Davis, George and Ira Gershwin, F. Scott Fitzgerald, Thomas Wolfe, and Ernest Hemingway (preferably all three as authors), and Ray Kroc, the man behind the McDonald's fast food restaurant chain.

3. For practice and active experience in using your imagination, choose at least three projects to work on. They can be anything you want and whatever interests you most. Just as an example, the three projects you select might be (1) a magazine article on any topic you wish, (2) a new way to increase productivity in your office, and (3) a new toy you invent for your son, daughter, or the kid down the street.

I'm sure you get the idea. What I'm stressing here is that you have and keep *three projects* going—all of which require you to use your imagination. Believe me when I say that the very best way to sharpen your imagination is to *use* it every day, or as often as you can each week. This will stretch the muscles of your imagination and keep it in tune.

Remember: *You* choose the projects you want to work on. They can be anything you like, just as long as they call for the use of your imagination. If and when you complete all three projects, go ahead and decide on three brand new ones. By always having such projects going, your imagination is bound to grow and sharpen.

4. Put your imagination to work on a problem you have . . . or answer you need. Your imagination may well solve a troublesome family, business, or personal problem. It has certainly done so for many others. But bear in mind that some time may be needed. Don't expect a breakthrough solution in hours or a few days. Thomas Edison had his imagination working on specific problems (such as the phonograph or electric light) for years before the right answers came.

Not long ago, I found myself thinking about writing a book about the legendary career of Elvis Presley. Everyone and his cousin has written an Elvis book, and I thought that I might do one, too, but from a different angle. I met him only once, but that's one more time than many of those who have been turning out Presley books.

So I put my imagination on the idea of an Elvis Presley book. In several weeks, I came up with the idea of having two newspaper men in a conversation about Elvis. The catch was, however, that these two newspaper men would be talking in their paper's office in the year 2005. August 16 (in 2005) would be nearing, and the Graceland mansion and estate, in Memphis, would be expecting several thousand people again to observe the twenty-eighth anniversary of Presley's death.

In other words, by using this idea, I would be showing, in a dramatic way, that the Elvis legend will still be alive and strong in the year 2005—some twenty-eight years after he died in 1977.

I liked this idea from my imagination very much and went to work on it. It turned out to be the first chapter in my book on Elvis. I haven't sold the project yet, mainly because so many books have already been published about him. But even if it doesn't sell, I *grew* from the experience of following through on this imaginative idea. I personally believe that more new Elvis books *will continue* to come out . . . at least for some years in the future, and possibly well into the 1990s. So I may sell my book sooner or later.

5. *Experiment* often with your imagination. By this I mean that you don't have to accept the first ideas you receive. Operate on the belief that the more answers, solutions, or ideas your imagination delivers, the better. You can then go over each of the possibilities and determine which ones seem to be the best. *There is quality in quantity* so the more results you get from your imagination, the more likely it is that some of them will be workable.

When you aren't satisfied with what your imagination delivers, go ahead and ask it for something better. That's right. Simply demand more from your imagination. Say something like this out loud several times a day: "Imagination, I know you can do better than this. I want and need better quality ideas, plans, solutions (or whatever)." This talking to yourself is okay if it improves the results. It might be wise not to go around in public addressing your imagination. But in the privacy of your home or office, I see nothing wrong with it. And I know that it works, as I've put through orders to my imagination many times over the years. I'm here to tell you that it's never let me down yet. It works at its own speed (and can't be rushed), and it delivers a higher quality at certain times than others. But it always delivers.

6. Recognize and accept the quality of *mystery* about the human imagination. Nobody really knows exactly how the imagination works. Where do the great ideas, for all manner of things, come from? What causes these ideas to pop into certain heads? There is a lot of mystery connected with it, and it's better to simply accept that fact. Be grateful for what your imagination brings you and try not to get hung up on the process itself. For imagination cannot be limited, or pinpointed, or described in an A-B-C way. It may work *differently* from day to day or week to week.

7. Try your imagination occasionally on some completely new field, area of interest, invention, product, creation, or what have you.

Author Judith Krantz was a free-lance magazine article writer for years before she turned her imagination loose on a first novel. Her imagination really came through for her and presented her the idea for *Scruples,* the story of a lovely girl from Boston who becomes an important name in the fashion world with her unique store called *Scruples.* Her first novel was a huge best seller.

In other words, don't feel that you have to confine your imagination to a *single* area, hobby, or interest alone. Give it full rein on occasion. Who knows? You may come up with some remarkable new idea or invention that will benefit millions of people. But whether you do or not, you will certainly see for yourself how your imagination can upgrade your personal life and daily work.

Refer to this chapter often as you develop and sharpen your imagination. Above all, keep three imaginative projects in the works at all times. When you achieve the current ones to your satisfaction, get three new ones underway as soon as possible.

Never forget that your imagination, once developed and actively used, can lift you to the very heights. It is far more important than just knowledge. It can definitely help you to rise above and overcome any feelings of disillusionment. Your imagination is *power.* Use it well for yourself . . . and to help and benefit others as well . . . for your imagination is magic.

Suggested Exercises
to Develop Your Imagination

1. A new electric product has been introduced by Northwest Electric Company of Mitchell, South Dakota. The product is a "devil dog" used to stop thieves and burglars on the spot.
Your Assignment: Use your imagination to invent a new product (the idea for it) to help people in the ongoing fight against crime.
2. A man in North Carolina decided that he wanted men without hair to enjoy life more. So he formed a club known as the Bald Headed Men of America. There are currently ninety-five hundred members in fifty states and twenty countries. The club holds a yearly convention. The philosophy of the club is summed up in their pamphlet: "The Lord is just. The Lord is fair. He gave some brains. And the others hair."
Your Assignment: Use your imagination to think up a *new* club that would have appeal for many people.
3. *The Never-Say-Diet Book* was a blockbuster best seller.
Your Assignment: Use your imagination to create the *idea* for a fresh new diet book (or safe system for losing weight).

You Must Always Have a Dream

You've heard of VIP power, vitamin power, money and political power, and so on. In this chapter, I want you to think about *dream power* and what it can do to change your life for the better.

Millions of people discover sooner or later that even the security of a job, career, or profession isn't enough. Many people, of course, go through the motions of each day's routine and maybe even claim to be reasonably satisfied. But deep down in the center of their beings, they know that something is missing. A dream can change that empty feeling, fill you with renewed vigor, and give you an ongoing reason for making the most of your time on earth.

What a Dream Can Do for You

Here are just a few of the advantages of having a dream in your life:

- A dream gives you a purpose, a reason for being, an objective.
- A dream stimulates your imagination and creativity.
- A dream keeps you more enthused about life in general.
- A dream motivates you to think ahead and plan for your future.
- Having a dream you are determined to fulfill can keep you more healthy. Medical experts have proven that boredom can actually kill you. A dream keeps you alive and humming on all cylinders.

- A dream enables you to get much more out of life in the way of personal satisfaction.
- A dream provides you with more overall zest for living.

Some Dreamers and the Dreams They Attained

There's an old saying that "brown eyes belong to dreamers." It's true, but the eyes of dreamers are also blue, hazel, green, and what have you. Anyone can dream, and millions do, but the great majority, unfortunately, let their dreams die too soon. They reason that the odds are too great against them realizing their dreams. So what happens? They give up much too soon; they throw in the towel and admit defeat. Possibly they never heard about the remark once made by General George S. Patton when a British general told him that a military move Patton already had underway "was impossible." Patton merely smiled at the general and replied that "the impossible is what we're in business for."

Take a look at some of the following dreamers who made their dreams come true, often in the face of overwhelming obstacles:

James Dean. The immortal actor had a tough time surviving in New York City, until he finally landed a part in a Broadway play. He even went back home to his native Indiana for brief visits, but he returned to Manhattan and kept trying. Eventually his career took off and Dean went on to motion picture fame and fortune. Short though his life was, he certainly achieved his dream.

George S. Patton. He vowed at age ten to become a great general one day. He fanned this dream with a white heat of desire and determination, and his objective became a vivid reality.

Anwar Sadat. He said that from a young age he felt he had some mission in life. When he later began to see it more clearly, Sadat made it come true and became a noble statesman of peace who changed the era in which he lived and the destiny of nations.

Dolly Parton. The queen of country music wanted to be a singer and songwriter. She learned the ropes in Nashville, built a name for herself, and enjoyed a number of hit records. But Dolly's dream

55

had a vaster horizon. She reached out for more, and in recent years, her career has broadened in other directions, with Las Vegas, films, and television bidding for her talent.

Lawrence Welk. Many people do not realize that the famous champagne music maker played all over the country . . . and for many years . . . before his style and sound of music caught on with the public. At this writing, Welk, now seventy-nine, has taped his last television program, saying that "it's time to quit." But his many shows already on tape will continue to be syndicated on television for several years to come. And the talented band leader may well be persuaded to return to the work he loves so much.

Paul Lynde. He dreamed of becoming a famous comedian and motion picture and television star. He actually sold his own blood in New York in order to stay alive while waiting for his first break. This alone shows remarkable determination to stick with a dream no matter what it takes. Lynde certainly made his dream come true and enjoyed a thirty-year career, attaining particularly great success as the main attraction of the television show "Hollywood Squares." Unfortunately, Lynde died in January 1982 at the age of fifty-five.

Marilyn Monroe. As a little girl, she stared out a window and dreamed of being on the silver screen some day. Through a series of small parts, she built a steadily rising name and film image. In "The Prince and the Showgirl," Marilyn proved that she had considerable acting talent. Though she died far too early, she left her footprints in a place of honor and did make her dream a reality.

How to Get Dream Power Going for You

Here are some proven guidelines for launching a dream of your own and making it become a reality:

1. If you don't now have a dream you would like to see come true, decide on what your major want, goal, or objective is. What is it that would make you very happy and bring you lasting fulfillment? You must try to come to grips with what it is, although most people, certainly the majority, are well aware of what their dreams are.

2. Write out a *clear* statement or description of your dream.

3. Start thinking about your dream a lot and develop an intense desire to achieve it.

4. Formulate a plan or series of steps you can take toward the fulfillment of your dream.

5. Work or move toward attaining the first step of your plan.

6. When you reach one step or goal of your plan, begin at once to head for the next one.

7. Remember each day that most people succeed by taking a lot of little steps. Like the saying goes, "Man succeeds by bits and pieces." Keep your eyes on one step or goal at a time and do all you can to get to that place in your plan. Once you arrive there, then you can set your sights on the next destination point of your plan.

8. Whenever you come across any item, idea, bit of advice, suggestion, guideline, pointer, or whatever that might help you move closer to your dream, write it down and try to use it, or make it a part of your plan. Over a period of years, you will discover and learn a lot of things that will help you make your dreams come true.

9. Visualize yourself as already having your dream. See yourself with the dream you want fulfilled, think how happy it will make you feel, and simply act like you've already realized it. This is pretending of course, but there is definite *power* in acting this way. This is the very way a great many have gotten the things they want and made their dreams (or at least some of them) come true.

10. Above all, each time you fulfill and make a dream a reality in your life, replace that realized dream with a *new* one. In other words, try to always have a dream you are trying to bring into reality. If you do this, your life will be far more exciting and interesting.

Dreams Do Come True

Finally, write these words in blazing red letters across the screen of your mind and in the central core of your being: *Dreams do come true.* Many people all over the world have experienced the unique thrill of realizing one or more important dreams in their lives. I see no reason why you cannot do the same. But you must know what your dream is, build a very strong desire to achieve it, work out a sensible plan for the steps, or series of goals leading to your dream, and then apply your plan relentlessly (plus updated, streamlined versions of your plan), regardless of the obstacles you may see in your pathway.

I'll be betting on you . . . and believing that you can and will make that dream in your heart a tangible reality. May you know that joyous moment of a dream fulfilled. There's nothing else quite like it.

Developing Your Inner Resources

The word has just come down. You've been sentenced to three-to-five years on Devil's Island, an escape-proof prison. Your appeals have all been denied, and it looks like your home for the next three years minimum is going to be a not-so-roomy cell on Devil's Island.

I posed such a fictional situation to some of my college-age communications students a few years back, and they found it to be quite interesting. In addition, I explained to them that the jailers on Devil's Island only allowed each one of them to bring *two items* with them, not counting a toothbrush and paste. Obviously, the two items could not be a file or any other tool useful in an escape attempt. Television sets were not permitted. The things selected by each inmate, then, had to be *reasonable* items.

After explaining the above situation, I asked for my students to name the two reasonable items each one of them would seriously wish to take with them, assuming they really were going to be in prison for three years on Devil's Island. I let them know in advance that I didn't expect any comic or humorous choices, no matter how tempted they might be to be funny.

I was fascinated with the papers I received on this discussion question. The unusual assignment proved to be very popular with my students because it gripped their attention and interest.

While reading over their papers, I quickly realized that most of them, as you might expect, had chosen *books* as their other two item choices. Here are some of their specific selections, as taken from their class papers:

1. *The Bible* and *Gone With the Wind*
2. *Appointment in Samarra* and *Gulliver's Travels*
3. *Treasure Island* and *Alice in Wonderland*
4. *Lorna Doone* and *To Kill a Mockingbird*
5. *Dynasty of Death* and *Moby Dick*
6. *Jaws* and *The Complete Short Stories of Edgar Allan Poe*
7. *The Grapes of Wrath* and *Jane Eyre*
8. *Two Years Before the Mast* and *Silas Marner*
9. *Kidnapped* and *Great Expectations*
10. *Wuthering Heights* and *A Tale of Two Cities*

As you might expect, many of the students included the *Bible* as one of the two items they would want to take. Others included dictionaries, history books, or encyclopedias.

Focusing on Your Inner Resources

I believe the Devil's Island example just described makes something very clear. Although most of us may never find ourselves behind bars in prison, there are times when disillusionment, disappointment, and unhappiness invade our lives. If you are able to draw on your *inner resources* during these difficult times, you will find it much easier to rise above the effects of disillusionment and overcome them.

By inner resources, I mean your developed ability to find happiness and contentment *within* yourself. Many people cannot be happy today because they seem to be too closely tied to and dependent on outer, material things, such as other people, flashy cars, gaudy clothes, money to spend on anything they want, diamonds, gourmet meals, and long visits in glamorous resorts to make them happy.

Such things are nice, but many people evidently can't live without them. If they no longer had them tomorrow morning, I doubt very much if these people would be able to cope with it. The reason they couldn't handle it is simply because they haven't developed enough inner resources to see them through the difficult periods of their lives. If and when these material goodies are swept away (no matter how they may go), the person who has sustained the losses is much better off if he or she is able to fall back on inner resources. These inner resources include the following:

• *An inner source of extra strength.* When Anwar Sadat was suddenly assassinated, his wife and family were faced with an enormous personal tragedy. The same thing was true for Prince Rainier, his two daughters, and son after the sudden car accident and death of Princess Grace. When these terrible events happen, they can be completely devastating to those loved ones left behind. Those who have developed a source of extra inner strength are more likely to be able to cope with such calamities.

• *The ability to bounce back from what life throws at you.* A good example here is the genial host and entertainer Bert Parks. When Parks was fired from his traditional job as host of the annual Miss America beauty contest, he took it in stride. In no time at all, an outraged nation stood up and spoke up for him. His good-natured personality and acceptance of his dismissal only made America angrier at the way he had been treated.

As the weeks and months passed, Bert Parks was absolutely flooded with offers to do commercials, episodes, and guest shot appearances. As he put it, "I'm overwhelmed at the offers I've received." But the point is that Parks wasn't rocked or done in by the firing. He had plenty of ability to bounce back quickly, becoming even more successful and in demand than he had been before.

• *The realization and wisdom that being by yourself doesn't have to mean loneliness.* Some people refer to this wisdom as self-contentment. It is a marvelous inner resource to have at your beck and call.

Self-contentment is simply the ability to be content, even happy, all by yourself. People find self-contentment in different ways, but one of the best is to have a place you can retreat to when you wish. It might be a snug little cabin way back in the woods or up in the mountains; perhaps it's a cottage near the lake.

Many people never have a cabin to get away to, yet they

remain self-content wherever they are. This is when self-content-ment can be a helpful inner resource. To be able to find comfort, peace, and contentment *within yourself* can be a great help all the way through life. It's like having a retreat, but you don't have to go anywhere. You're already there. You simply enter the retreat based within yourself.

• *Hope for the future, no matter how dark the present may seem.* To maintain the flame of hope in spite of everything is to be a stubborn and optimistic person. The world needs more of such people.

When the months continued to stretch into a year for the American hostages held in Iran, many of them refused to give up hope that one day they would be both free and home again. That hope nourished and sustained them during their long and often trying ordeal.

"Sixty Minutes," the popular television news magazine show, reported last July on how three key employees were fired by a department store chain. Those fired claimed that the reason for their termination was so that the company could get out of paying pensions. One of the employees had run the most profitable divi-sion of the store chain. The three former employees filed suit and won a whopping $1.9 million settlement, but the chain store is appealing the decision and vows to take the case all the way to the Supreme Court. Meanwhile, the three fired employees had to find new jobs. They refused to give up hope. At this writing, all three have found new jobs. One man went into real estate, one woman got a job as a manager in another department store, and the third employee, a man, is running a carnation farm.

Whatever your needs may be—for a job, food, security, a friend, someone to love, or whatever, never lose hope. For hope is always better and wiser than despair. Hope can keep you going, while despair makes you want to lie down and give up.

• *The ability to amuse, entertain, or stay interested on your own.* Millions of people would be at a loss for what to do and how to entertain themselves if their television sets were gone tomorrow. They have grown dependent on the tube for their free time entertainment.

During the late 1920s, when Margaret Mitchell had to stay in bed for several years for health reasons, she certainly made the most of that period of her life. To amuse herself, she wrote about Atlanta, the Civil War, and lost herself in the fascination of creating characters like Scarlett O'Hara, Rhett Butler, Ashley and Melanie Wilkes, and all the rest. She never thought or even considered the possibility of publication for her work. She worked on it for one reason—her own interest and amusement. It was years later, after a Macmillan editor heard about her work and came to Atlanta, that *Gone With the Wind* was published (in 1936).

• *Self-control for those times in your life when you're tempted to lose your temper, be impatient, or jump to conclusions.* Some persons have little or no self-control, so when something happens that angers or upsets them, they just cannot handle it.

There may be one or more difficult people in the place where you work or individuals you are forced to deal with who are hard to get along with. You need self-control at such times and the sure knowledge, or assurance, that "this, too, will pass."

A Test on Your Present Inner Resources

Answer the following questions with either a YES or NO, and then add up your score. If you're not sure about a particular question, go with the answer it seems to lean toward or indicate. An evaluation of your score follows the test, but you should not look it over until after you've answered the following questions:

		YES	NO
1.	Can you entertain and amuse yourself when you're alone?	___	___
2.	Do you mind being alone for fairly long periods of time?	___	___
3.	If you lost your job tomorrow, do you think you would be devastated by it?	___	___
4.	When everything seems to be going poorly for you, do you feel discouraged and like giving up?	___	___
5.	Do you have a basic philosophy of life (an overall view or statement of your own values and beliefs)?	___	___

How to Score Your Test

Questions one and five should have been answered with a YES. Questions two through four should have been answered with a NO. Give yourself twenty points for each question you answered correctly and place your total score here: _____

Remember: This little test is just an *indication* of your present inner resources. It is certainly not the last word. You may well have inner resources you are unaware of, and perhaps this little test will help you to see their importance and urge you to develop them more.

EVALUATION OF YOUR SCORE

Score	Meaning
100	Your inner resources are presently in strong working order.
80	Your inner resources are in healthy condition, but they can be strengthened.
60	Your inner resources need more development.
40	You have little or no inner resources on which to draw.

As you seek to develop your inner resources, refer back to this chapter. Take one resource, such as hope for the future, and strive to develop it much more in your life. When you feel that you've developed it to a stronger level, move on to another resource. In this way, you'll be focusing all your attention and efforts on a single resource at a time. Here are some suggestions to help you:

1. Try to spend more time with people who seem to have an abundance of the particular resource you're trying to develop.
2. Use positive statement affirmations each morning and evening. Here's an example: "Every day, in every way, I'm becoming a more hopeful person."
3. Determine in your mind what you can do to get more of a certain resource going for you. For example, to develop more self-control, you might resolve to cool off for five or ten minutes, to count to one hundred, to leave the scene temporarily, or other possibilities when you are angered.
4. Start a regular period of meditation each day (or night) during which you concentrate exclusively on the resource you wish to

develop. This step is a definite way to increase the resources you want. It works.

5. Project yourself into the future and actually see, in your mind's eye, more of the resources you want. In other words, visualize yourself as a stronger person; or one with more self-contentment, self-control, hope; ability to bounce back, to entertain and amuse yourself; and so on. You might even devise tests for yourself. The next time you find yourself snowed in, test yourself to see if you can amuse and entertain yourself for long periods of time. Anything that exercises the resource you want more of will be of help.

Your
Spiritual Life
Can Sustain You

10

With millions of people everywhere feeling so disillusioned these days, doomsters in Chicago and elsewhere stockpiling food, the economy jitters, crime soaring through the roof, and more people than ever before believing that we are indeed living in the last days, you and I both need all the encouragement, help, and sustenance we can get. That's what this chapter is meant to do for you—show you the importance of a regular spiritual life and how to get one going and maintain it.

The Importance of a Spiritual Life

Spiritual values have taken quite a nosedive in recent years, and this in itself is a major reason for taking the time for a regular spiritual program. A retired Georgia Methodist bishop put his finger on the pulse of this national problem when he stated that "along the walls of this republic is the handwriting of God." Spiritual values are at a low ebb. According to this bishop, "Americans have been putting cash value above conscience. Without a spiritual awakening, this country is not going to survive this difficult time, for when faith begins to die, all other things die."

At 11:30 one morning in New York, a Kentucky businessman witnessed a blood-chilling sight. While walking down the street, he happened to look up and see a young lady ready to jump from a ninth story window. Nobody was near her, and no voice yelled in restraint. Before this executive could even say anything or cry out for help, the woman jumped. He found out later that she was only thirty.

But what was worse than her jump to the pavement below was the *cold* and *careless* reaction of the people as they realized what had happened. Curious at first, many in the crowd didn't even slow down as they passed right by the scene. The Kentucky executive described how routinely and heartlessly the police ambulance orderlies removed her body on a stretcher . . . and how they kept cracking jokes the entire time.

In a mere ten minutes, the pavement where the woman had hit was washed and dried, and hundreds of people continued on their hectic rush. As the executive later reacted, "It made me feel very sad, and it makes you wonder just how cheap human life is anyway—especially in a cold, heartless large city."

Here are some of the key reasons why a regular and continual spiritual life is important:

1. A regular, ongoing spiritual life can help, or certainly influence, one to be a more caring, understanding, thoughtful, forgiving, less selfish, and loving person.
2. Most of us, as human beings, need a *continual relationship* with God (or as some prefer to say, a higher power).
3. A spiritual life adds purpose and meaning to life.
4. A spiritual life provides Christian *fellowship* with friends and loved ones, who may be as disillusioned as we are and also trying to find their way. A *sense of sharing* is thus often realized.
5. A spiritual life can be a direct and dependable source of comfort, joy, and peace.

The Nature
of a Spiritual Life

A spiritual life usually includes most, or all, of the following:

- An ongoing prayer life
- Regular periods of meditation and thoughtful contemplation

69

- The establishment of a regular worship program through daily or weekly attendance at chapel, church services, or Mass
- Commemoration of the Lord's Supper
- A continuous study of the Scriptures
- A persistent effort to live your faith *throughout the week* and in accord with the Ten Commandments

The Actress Who Responded to a Higher Calling

Dolores Hart was a beautiful young actress who left Hollywood twenty years ago, in the prime of her career, to become a Roman Catholic nun.

She had it all—looks, talent, and a booming film career. Yet she packed her things, told her fiancé and many friends goodbye, and caught a plane. Her parting words expressed gratitude: "I'm taking a grateful heart with me."

She had been one of the most popular young actresses in the late 1950s and early 1960s, appearing in such films as *Loving You* (with Elvis Presley), *Where the Boys Are, King Creole, Lisa,* and *Come Fly With Me.*

Dolores was born a Protestant but converted to the Catholic faith at age ten. While a freshman at Marymount College, she went to a dance at Loyola University and met a boy who asked her to play the lead in an all-student production of "Joan of Lorraine."

This same friend sent pictures of Dolores, as Joan in the play, to various Hollywood producers. Hal Wallis liked her photos and signed her to a movie contract. Even then, at only nineteen, she was more serious-minded than most girls her age. As she herself said at the time: "I'm probably too serious. But I have a goal set on many things."

The popular actress was on the verge of marriage before deciding to accept a higher calling. It was no snap decision though. She thought about it for some time before reaching her final decision in 1963. Her many friends were heartbroken to see her leave the film colony. Her high ideals and strong character brought strength to those who knew and worked with her. She was a bright ray of sunshine on the Hollywood scene. But she was sure. She had

70

visited the monastery a number of times before, while appearing in a Broadway play.

Dolores took her final vows well over ten years ago. The ceremony came only after a number of years of prayer and study. Her daily schedule is very busy and often exhausting, but she still finds the time to write to her friends in Hollywood. There were those who predicted and hoped she wouldn't stick to her life as a nun, but she has.

She doesn't consider herself cut off from the world and its people. In fact, she believes she is now even closer to those she left behind: "The silence of God is the sound of the heartbeat of all humanity. We here in the monastery are attempting to speak to all of you, every day of your lives."

Some of her friends still feel that her role as Saint Clare, in the film *Saint Francis of Assisi,* may have been at least one influence on her eventual decision to devote her life completely to God as a nun. Clare, in the film, is so moved by the preachings of Saint Francis that she renounces the worldly life and becomes a nun.

Her life at the monastery is not without some relaxation. The nuns are allowed a period for recreation in the evening. They talk to one another and enjoy each other's company at this time. There are other set periods for work, rest, prayer, study, and indoor or outdoor solitude.

All the Benedictine nuns assemble seven times a day to sing praises of God. It's called the Divine Office. With all their duties, Dolores and the other nuns still also find time to take part in arts and crafts programs, embroidery, ceramics, painting, cooking, sewing, and other activities.

Since the day she left Hollywood many years ago, friends and fans of Dolores have speculated as to how and why she could leave it all behind—fame, fortune, her many friends and loved ones, and a wonderful, booming career. Yet, ever since she was a little girl, she was very religious. She once said that she wasn't afraid of living, "but of living without a purpose."

So a new sense of purpose can do much to lift you out of the ranks of the disillusioned. As for Dolores, it's refreshing and inspiring to know of someone who felt and responded to a higher calling—someone who wanted to live closer to the deeper, spiritual values and realities.

The Soldier Who Took A Stand
for Spiritual Values

In action with the enemy near Chateau-Thierry, France in 1918, Sergeant Alvin York assumed command after his platoon had suffered heavy casualties. Leading seven men, York charged a machine-gun nest that was cutting down his platoon. While putting the machine gun out of action, the amazing York also captured four officers, 132 men, and several guns.

In presenting the Medal of Honor to York, Major General Duncan said of him: "Such deeds are evidence of that spirit and heroism which is innate in the highest type of American soldier and responds unfailingly to the call of duty wherever or whenever it may come." Marshall Foch, commander-in-chief of the allied forces, decorated York with the Croix de Guerre, saying to him, "What you did was the greatest thing ever accomplished by any soldier of any of the armies of Europe."

Returning from overseas a world hero, York was given a ticker-tape parade in New York, was met by admirals, generals, congressmen, and many celebrities. He was offered a fortune to lend his name to advertisements and various promotions. York refused with this reply: "This uniform is not for sale." He later explained his feelings further: "I was offered many different kinds of positions, and tonight I could have $500,000 in the bank if I had accepted those offers. But I read in a little book I carried on the battlefields of France something that I remembered. It said, 'What does it profit a man if he gains the whole world and loses his own soul?' When I came back here, I remembered that those little ones in the mountains were struggling for something greater than money—the right to become upright and Christian men and women— and I thought I would show them the example."

When York arrived back in Nashville in May 1919, some six thousand people gave him an ovation at Ryman Auditorium. The people of Tennessee gave him a farm near his former home. The commercial offers kept pouring in, but York kept refusing them, including movie, stage, and lecture offers.

In answer to the numerous tributes paid him, York once said, "America is the only nation that has the greatest generation of young men; let's make it a better nation and a more Christian nation. Let's better the towns and cities, but first let's better ourselves."

York married his childhood sweetheart in 1919. A York Foundation was established at his request, in order to support both a local Bible school and an industrial school. York gave part of his royalties from *Sergeant York,* the hit film of 1941, to the foundation.

York was buried with full military honors near his home in Pall Mall, Tennessee, in September 1964. In an official statement on the death of York, Army Chief of Staff General Harold K. Johnson stated: "Sergeant York was a great citizen-soldier who symbolized the infantry rifleman at his finest for three generations of Americans. High moral courage and steadfast devotion to *spiritual values* characterized his military service and his later civilian pursuits. In this way he wrote a new chapter in the legend of the American fighting man that must stand forever as an example of man's greatest glory—the placing of life itself at the service of others."

Truths Revealed
Through the Spiritual Life

Here are just a few of the essential truths that are revealed through a regular and ongoing spiritual life:

- The universe is still in God's hands. God is going to have the last word. He controls the end of history.
- In Jesus Christ, we know something of God's character. We know his consistent love.
- The Christian does not have to struggle to earn salvation. God has given him this, and he is now free to proclaim the Lordship of Christ over all reality.
- The Christian has no need to be pessimistic about history. There are times when the forces of evil seem to dominate life, but there are no ideologies, totalitarian states, or dictators that can stand up to the King of Kings.
- Part of the joy of being a Christian is to live and work in the world that is ruled by God, our heavenly Father.

How to Develop and Maintain
a Spiritual Program

By following a number of directions and suggestions, you can start, develop, and maintain a spiritual life program of your own. Here are some suggestions to help you:

- Attend a retreat center for prayer and contemplation. Most churches and religious organizations can provide you with information on these retreats offered during each year. Your attendance at such retreats a few times a year can be of real help.
- Strive to maintain a regular prayer life.
- Try reading the Bible all the way through. This can easily be done by determining to read just one chapter each morning or evening.
- Keep up with new inspirational books being published and read those of your choice. Such books, along with the Bible, can be of enormous help to you in rising above disillusionment.
- Realize the blessings in your life and be grateful for what you do have. Try to do your best with what you have . . . and in the place where you now are.
- When you pray, ask for, and expect, direction and guidance for your future.
- Take an active part in the ongoing work and activities of your church or religious organization.
- Seek, if possible, to help someone else along the way. For in helping others, we help ourselves.

Allow for
the Unexpected

11

Today's world is a troubled one. You see evidence of it in your daily newspaper and on the evening news. Many people have quit watching the evening television news because it's so depressing. Mark Twain once said that the happiest time in his life "was a period of seven years when he didn't pick up a newspaper."

Many people believe that the world is off its hinges and speeding toward a cliff, much like a runaway car. Millions are troubled both in mind and spirit. They're disillusioned. They feel engulfed by a sense of helplessness.

Assassinations, corruption in high places, worry about the economy, the soaring crime rate, shortages of one kind or another, the nuclear build-up, mad people who poison headache tablets, and the unbelievable greed for money and power have all, collectively, caused countless numbers of people to feel anxious, nervous, disillusioned, and very troubled indeed.

A Peace Beyond All Understanding

The greatness of God demands peace for the troubled mind and spirit. A closer relationship with God can and will bring you more peace in this life and fill your mind with the assurance that God still has everything under control.

When Christ returns to earth, the world will know the full meaning of this peace, which passes all understanding. God wants all of His troubled children to have this kind of peace, and one day we will know it in its fullness.

To find much of this peace for our everyday here and now lives, God continually speaks to each of us. "Be still, and know that I am God." He asks you to believe Him, trust Him, give Him the reins of your life, follow Him, and He will give you not only peace, but also a crown of salvation and eternal life. And it will be life with no more pain, sadness, grief, heartache, or death.

The Unexpected May Strike at Anytime

Part of what troubles many people is the unexpected. The unexpected strikes when you least expect it. It struck a savage arrival at Pearl Harbor on December 7, 1941. You can visit the monument there to the U.S.S. *Arizona*. The ship is still listed on the records. With all her crew, the *Arizona* certainly faced the sudden and unexpected that tragic morning.

Life is full of the unexpected. It troubles people everywhere. The question is what do *you* do when the unexpected strikes? Do you waver in the wind or stand firm? As long as you're in this world, you will be faced with the possible unexpected. The same is true for every other human being. But the words of Jesus are most comforting: "You will find trouble in the world, but fear not; I have overcome the world." And there are other sources of comfort in God's holy word: "God is our refuge and strength, a very present help in trouble."

Facing the Unexpected

There's a difference between how the non-Christian and the Christian face the unexpected. What does the non-Christian, or the one-time Christian who has drifted away, have to fall back upon? What sources of aid are available? There is, of course, the person's resourcefulness, including his or her courage, determination, or abilities to find a solution. Such a person may have friends or relatives

77

to turn to for help. If so, then this type of individual is not without resource. But without the foundation of a faith, the conviction that there *is meaning* in life, that there is purpose to back up one's positive qualities, will there not be a drag eventually on one's physical or mental powers?

How does one face an unexpected crucial moment? Say, for example, that a non-Christian and a Christian are sitting beside each other as the plane they are on goes into a sudden dive, apparently about to crash. Now every Christian in such a position might not face such a moment with victorious calm, but isn't the Christian much better equipped as he or she plunges toward the earth? In such moments, even the staunchest Christian could break, or panic, and even the worst sinner could truly ask God to forgive him and mean it. But either way, a lot depends on the particular person's relationship with God. The type of crucial moment that a person faces, then, depends on whether he or she thinks they can face it with his or her power or must call upon God.

Degrees and Qualities
of the Unexpected

There are, of course, degrees and qualities of the unexpected. Some don't seem too difficult or complicated, and we can often cope with them. But just as nobody knows if he or she will be in an auto accident (and therefore whether or not to use a seat belt), nobody really knows how serious the future unexpected may be and if he or she can handle it alone.

Well-known stars of film, stage, and records sometimes suddenly find their day in the spotlight has gone or has been greatly dimmed. The unexpected has struck again. It may have been taking place gradually, without the person accepting the truth. Or it may seemingly happen overnight.

The unexpected may be something inspiring on occasion. Not long ago, a former newspaper promotions editor in the South resigned to devote full time to an evangelistic career. It was the unexpected for his friends, his employer, and apparently even his family.

The people laughed as they watched Noah build an ark to

preserve his household in safety. The message God gave to Noah may have at first seemed foolish to Noah, too, but he believed and trusted God. Noah and his family were saved. The flood came, and it was entirely unexpected by the disbelievers who had laughed at the old man and his family.

Think of Abraham launching out, with no idea of where he was heading. He was willing to face the unexpected because of his confidence and deep trust in God.

So realize that a major source of your troubles comes from the unexpected. But as long as you're in this world, you must stand your ground and cope with it as best you can. Reading the Bible, prayer, and a close relationship with God can help you face whatever the future may hold. Being close to God on a daily basis can help you cope with disillusionment, loneliness, life's many irritations, worries, difficult people, uptight feelings, personal problems, emotional stresses, and so on right down the line of human troubles.

Think of and Understand God in Three Specific Ways

A greater sense of peace for anyone who is troubled may also be derived by understanding God in three particular ways. One way is to think of God as the originator and creator of not only the universe, but everything in it as well. This thought in itself will give you a sense of calm and peace. It's much like the hit song of years ago said it—"He's Got the Whole World in His Hands."

Secondly, think of God and understand Him as your redeemer. You and I were bought with a price—the voluntary giving of the Son of God. By believing this, you are justified through Christ, who first loved us and gave Himself for us. God has saved us, if we will accept His redemption.

Finally, understand and think of God as the best friend you can possibly have. Strive to develop a closer relationship with Him. Ask Him to hold the reins of your life and to lead you according to His will. Ask Him to become your senior partner, and your work, job, or career will take on a fresher meaning than you have ever known before.

As you grow closer to God through Christ, you will find yourself wanting to improve. You will seek more goodness, honor, truth, and lasting spiritual values. You will desire to make the world a better place, if only a little, because you passed this way.

As a child of God, you are an heir of His peace, which passes understanding. You can know a greater degree of this peace right here on earth through prayer, worship, a study of His word, and a closer relationship with Him. Some of the ideas in this chapter will help you accomplish a closer relationship. And in the greater life beyond this one, you will know the full meaning of His peace.

So "let not your heart be troubled," whether because of disillusionment or whatever. His peace will be yours. You have the power within you, through your personal faith, to handle anything and everything the unexpected may throw at you.

Get Into Work You Can Love

12

Happy is the woman or man who loves his work. Any person who loves his or her work will not be disillusioned for very long, for happiness in one's work is one of life's richest blessings. It keeps you renewed and enthused for the work activities and pursuits of each new day.

Would You Be Happier in Some Other Work?

Take the following short test to see if you might be happier in some other line of work. Score ten points for each correct answer. An evaluation of your test score follows the questions:

	YES	NO
1. Do you find it difficult to work on Mondays?	____	____
2. Does your mind frequently wander off the work at hand?	____	____
3. Is the most important thing about the work you do the paycheck you receive?	____	____
4. Do you occasionally dream of being in another line of work?	____	____

	YES	NO

5. Do you sometimes wish you could change places with a friend, neighbor, or relative . . . and be in *his* or *her* field of work? ____ ____

6. Do you believe that a job or career change might be one of the smartest decisions a person can make? ____ ____

7. Have you ever described the work you are now doing as a "dead end job?" ____ ____

8. Would you agree with the following statement: There are too many round pegs in square holes. ____ ____

9. In your opinion, would the loss of some fringe benefits be worth the chance to be in another line of work more to your liking? ____ ____

10. Do you occasionally or often feel that your talents, abilities, and interests indicate that you would do better in some other field of work and like it a great deal more? ____ ____

EVALUATION OF YOUR TEST SCORE

Score ten points for each question you answered YES and zero for each one you responded to with a NO. Then add up your score and place the total here: _____

Score	Meaning
90 to 100	This high score shows that you are certainly not happy in your present work. You should definitely seek to get into other work more to your liking.
80 to 90	There is good reason to believe that you should try to make a change to more suitable work.
70 to 80	This score means that you are *fairly unhappy* in your present line of work. You would probably be happier doing something else.
60 to 70	There is very little reason, judging by this score, to seek a change in your position.
50 to 60	Forget about making a switch. You should most likely stay where you are.

As you have no doubt guessed or realized long ago, the *truth* is that few people really love the work they do. But that's no reason for not *trying* to get into work you can love. This nation is still considered by most to be a free country, and that means you have the perfect right, as well as a responsibility to yourself, to seek to find the work you would be happiest doing . . . and hopefully the work you could love.

Examples of People
Who Love Their Work

Here are a number of examples of people from various walks of life. All of them have one thing in common. They loved or still love their work:

Bob Hope	Bob is an American treasure. Every time he appears and walks out on a stage, he shows how much he loves his work. It isn't work at all for Bob. It's his life.
Arthur Fiedler	The late conductor of the Boston Pops radiated his great love for his work each time he picked up the baton.
Rich Little	The genius of impersonation loves what he does, and it always shows. He couldn't stop doing his amazing impressions if he wanted to.
William F. Buckley	The host of "Firing Line" and frequent television guest on other shows loves all phases of his career and work—from magazine editing, hosting his own show, and writing.
James, the man who takes care of my lawn	This still-robust man of eighty-three years loves his work, consisting of doing odd jobs and taking care of a number of lawns. He loves being able to still do his work.
A Midsouth pet store manager	This woman's love for dogs, cats, and other animals shows in her positive attitude and enthusiasm for finding just the right pet for each customer.

A sales rep for a major New York publisher	There's no doubt that this young and attractive woman is in love with her career. She loves reading, in advance, all the new books her company publishes and then presenting each, on its merits, to the bookstore customers she calls on.
Billy Graham	It's been obvious for years that the popular evangelist loves his work and feels that he is accomplishing something important for God (though Graham takes no personal credit for it).
Ruth Gordon	Actress, writer, and entertainer Ruth Gordon is still going strong at 85. She absolutely refuses to slow down, which is one sign of a love for one's work. As Ruth puts it, "I don't believe in being idle. I have a helluva lot of ideas. What would I do with them if I didn't follow them up?"
John Wilbur	My brother, a successful lawyer in Florida, loves his work very much. The challenge, interest, dedication, and goal of doing his best for each client is clearly revealed when he relates and describes various legal cases. It's no wonder to me and to the rest of his family that each client of his firm wants him to handle their legal work *personally*.
Chris Evert Lloyd	The love this tennis champion has for the game is clearly evident. To start playing as young as most of the pros do shows a strong love indeed for the sport.

Winning Against the Odds

Whenever you feel engulfed with a sense of disillusionment, read over the following inspiring message. It can certainly help you to snap back, find the right work for you, and rise within it. At the very least, it shows that even with tremendous odds against you, it's still very possible to go places in life. Like someone once said, "Impossible is the adjective of fools." Some people who know about this message claim to have read it over thousands of times. Here are the words:

WINNING AGAINST THE ODDS

"Cripple him, and you have a Sir Walter Scott.
Lock him in a prison cell, and you have a John Bunyan.
Bury him in the snows of Valley Forge, and you
have a George Washington.
Raise him in abject poverty, and you have an Abraham Lincoln.
Subject him to bitter religious prejudice, and you have a Disraeli.
Afflict him with asthma as a child, and you
have a Theodore Roosevelt.
Stab him with rheumatic pains until he can't sleep without an
opiate, and you have a Steinmetz.
Put him in a grease pit of a locomotive roundhouse, and you have a
Walter P. Chrysler.
Make him second fiddle in an obscure South American orchestra,
and you have a Toscanini."

(Source unknown)

Make
Someone Else
Happy

13

Happiness is a perfume you can't pour on others without getting some on yourself. Those persons who have tested and practiced this concept have found that it is quite true. Like the pop song of past vintage years set it to music, "Make someone happy, then you will be happy too."

The sad thing that came across to me in what turned out to be Pierre Sallinger's last interview with the late and lovely Princess Grace, was the feeling, or impression, that she had not been really happy in recent years. She had plenty of wealth, atmosphere, and all the trimmings and accessories of the royal life, but was she really happy? I don't think so. As Grace admitted herself, she resented the lack of privacy for her children, even though she had long ago accepted that her private life became public when she married in 1956.

Millions of people everywhere think that wealth, a beautiful place to live, and a truly royal life would ensure anyone's happiness. Not necessarily. It's no definite *guarantee* of happiness, which is more of an inner feeling. Perhaps the truth about Princess Grace lies in the statement made by Pierre Salinger on television, when his interview with Grace was shown on ABC's "20-20" program: "She wasn't as happy as many people thought."

Movies That Give You a Lift

Up until the release of the hit film *E.T.* I had reached the conclusion that Hollywood was through turning out films that left people with a happy and positive feeling.

There were exceptions of course. *The Sound of Music* was one. It brought happiness to many people. Another one, *That's Entertainment* (both parts one and two), did the same.

More than any other film studio, M-G-M became known and is still remembered for its top quality musicals. A young Dennis Morgan started it in a spectacular musical of the late 1930s. From there on, stars like Fred Astaire, Eleanor Powell, Jimmy Durante, Gene Kelly, Donald O'Connor, Judy Garland, and other names of the 1940s and 1950s blended their talents to bring unforgettable musical gems to the screen. Such fantasy musicals meant a lot to Americans during the trying war years and offered an entertaining means of escape.

Think of Walt Disney and his dedicated objective of bringing happiness to millions of moviegoers. He certainly achieved that goal with four-star quality films still remembered by millions.

Making Others Happy

Here are some suggestions for bringing happiness to others along the way:

1. Take a gift to a friend or shut-in you know about. It may well be the highlight of the week or month for the person you visit.
2. Throw a surprise birthday or congratulations party for someone in your life.
3. Get the names of members of your church or religious affiliation who are sick in the hospital, and go to see them. Just the fact that you remembered them will be a tonic for these ill people. A hospital can be a terribly dreadful and lonely place.
4. Pick out just the right greeting card for someone and send it.
5. Create something that you feel would bring a lift to others. It may be a poem, story, article, song, or book. Put something of yourself or ideas that will help people into it. You may well have the ability

to create something that will inspire many people out there. People are happier when they feel inspired.

6. Take a book to someone you know. Choose a book that has meant a lot to you, one you believe can brighten the life of someone else.

7. If you know an elderly person who lives alone, take that person a pet (perhaps a dog or cat). Doctors now say that a pet can change a sad and lonely person's outlook considerably. The pet accepts the person regardless of his or her age and physical limitations. Pets can become a substitute for people. They bring happiness to millions.

8. Try giving of yourself in this way: Find someone in need of help and then lend a hand. It may be by paying a bill, helping with a college expense, or just the price of a meal. There are lots of people out there in need.

9. Try to encourage someone you know (who is unhappy) to join a positive thinking group. The idea is to get the person interested and taking part in the various activities of the club . . . and meeting others.

10. Organize a new group or club yourself. Make the purpose of your group to do all you can, individually and collectively, to bring happiness to others. This goal might be reflected in dinner parties for various people, outings, sharing of sports activities, baking cakes and cookies to take to people, visits to individuals, and so on.

Making Others Happy
Dissolves Your Disillusionment

Bringing some happiness into the lives of others can melt away your personal disillusionment. It has certainly done this for a great many.

Many years ago, I was a young sailor feeling lonely and unhappy in New York. My ship, in Boston, was leaving the next day for a long, eight-month cruise and tour of duty in the Mediterranean. I wandered into the New York Public Library that Saturday afternoon, thinking that reading something would cheer me up. It did. I read about a national song contest being held by a magazine. I decided for the rest of the afternoon that I would try to come up with a lyric. I had never tried to write a song before. I couldn't seem to get any ideas. But then I thought about how many millions of people there must be all over the world who were far more unhappy than I. Why not try to write a song for them, a song to cheer them up and give them hope?

Some three hours later, I had finished a lyric. I polished it up until I felt I couldn't improve it anymore. Later, on the way back to my ship, I dropped the lyric into the mail as my entry in the song contest. I forgot all about it during the next eight months overseas.

When I got back home and was on leave, I opened a letter one day at home and read that my lyric had won the national song contest sponsored by the magazine. My winning lyric was there in print, in the magazine, and I received mail from famous and un-known composers from all over the country. All of them wanted to do the music for my lyric. I later agreed to let a New York composer do the music, and the result was a beautiful ballad. The song has been performed many times and led me into songwriting, which has brought me a great deal of personal happiness and pleasure over the years. A number of my songs have been published, re-corded, and performed. And several even won other national awards.

But above all, I learned something on that bleak day in New York, working over a lyric in the public library. I learned that by sincerely trying to help others, you can rise above your feelings of unhappiness and disillusionment. When I returned to my ship that night, I had forgotten all about unhappiness. I felt elated, uplifted, and fascinated over the experience of creating a song (even though just a lyric at the time) that had never existed before. Here is the song I wrote that day:

THERE'S STILL TOMORROW

There's Still Tomorrow
If things go wrong today
There's still a rainbow
Beyond those clouds of gray

Don't be downhearted
Just hold your head up high
And keep on smiling
As life goes passing by.

91

Make Someone Else Happy

They say we're all just actors
Upon this stage called life
We play our roles, the good and bad
Grateful for the parts we've had

There's Still Tomorrow
If things go wrong today
You'll find your rainbow
Beyond those clouds of gray.

Be Yourself:
You're an Original

14

Back in my junior high school days, I had great fun appearing in a talent show. I sang a then very popular song called "The Girl That I Marry." The way I sang the song evidently reminded those in the audience of Frank Sinatra, and I still remember one of my teachers saying that "it's far better to develop your own original style . . . rather than to sound like someone else." I did not consciously try to sound like Sinatra, but that song was associated with him.

I never forgot what my teacher said, and I think it's still a valid point. Whatever you try to do and no matter what the field may be, it's certainly wiser to blaze your own trail, to be original, to do something in your very own way.

Consider the following facts about yourself:

1. There is nobody else *just like you* anywhere. They say that someone, somewhere, may resemble each of us—a person who looks like you—but in other respects the odds are great that you're unique.

2. Your ideas, viewpoints, and opinions are yours alone. They are representatives of your particular personality.

3. You have talents and abilities that are right for *you*. The degree to which you develop and use them is up to you.

4. The pathway you take in life is your personal choice. The decisions and choices you make through the years are yours alone (unless you allow others to influence you).

You can easily see that nobody lives the same life as someone else. Your life is different because you, yourself, are different.

James Dean, Elvis, and Marilyn Were Originals

Once in awhile an original comes along who astounds the world. James Dean was certainly one in the entertainment field. He made only three films, but *East of Eden, Rebel Without a Cause,* and *Giant* added up to a considerable contribution. Dean was only twenty-four when he died in an auto accident, but he had touched a responsive chord in millions by that early age. Millions of young people of that era *identified* with him and saw themselves in Dean's sensitiveness and search to find love and happiness.

The same is true of Elvis Presley. He was a highly *original* star who blazed his way into the hearts and lives of his era. At this writing, the record industry is hurting. Sales have dropped over a billion dollars. "The industry needs a new sound, a new vital force to put new life into it," said a recording executive recently.

Music also needed a new sound and excitement during the middle 1950s. And Elvis provided it with his unique rock-and-roll gift to the industry. There was nobody else like him then or now, despite the numerous look-alike Elvis impersonators who have cropped up since his death.

Flashback to the early 1960s: Marilyn Monroe is up there on the screen singing "I'm Through With Love," in the popular film, *Some Like It Hot.* No other actress looked, sang, or acted like her. Marilyn took the movie world by storm. She was unique . . . another original.

Don't think for a moment that this originality is confined to movie stars and the entertainment world in general. There are original and gifted people in *all walks* of life. You just don't hear about them. They don't get the publicity, attention, and world spotlight given to movie stars and entertainment celebrities.

Ulrich Inderbinen, for example, at eighty-two is the world's oldest mountain guide. He is still very active in his work and guides visitors regularly to lofty peaks of more than twelve thousand feet. Ulrich lives in Switzerland and has been a mountain guide for over fifty-eight years. I am sure it would be difficult indeed to find someone just like Ulrich—someone with his years of experience, views, ideas, and beliefs.

Your Originality
Is a Marvelous Treasure

I urge you to cherish and value highly your originality. Here are some directions along these lines:

• Be *suspicious* of new ideas you receive (in any field), regardless of how original they may seem to be. A good example here is the experience shared by many songwriters. Sometimes they believe they have created a fine new melody, only to discover a bit later that the music already exists. They were tapping in on already known music.

• Encourage your spark of originality by being receptive to new innovations, ideas, methods, systems, or whatever. Let your mind know that you *appreciate* its productivity.

• Always be alert to signs of originality in your daily life, whether it comes via other people, television, books, magazines, business reports, seminars, or what have you. You could even keep an ongoing collection of what you feel are strong or worthy examples of originality. Then study those examples when you can.

• Write out a personal statement of how you define originality . . . or the art of being original. A clear understanding of it can only help you to recognize it whenever you see it.

• Realize at all times that being yourself is a *must* for originality. In other words, don't try to be a carbon copy of someone else in business, at your job or profession, at school, in running your home, the office, or wherever. Your best chance—the real opportunities—will come from being true to yourself, your inner visions, ideas, ways of thinking, seeing, or doing something. Why copy or walk in another person's footprints? Your *own* way in your own style is what you should seek. If you copy another, your identity becomes lost or confused. *Your* originality may well prove to be of much more importance and value than what you might achieve by simply copying others.

If you speak before a group, do it *your* way. If you write an article, business report, theme paper, office memo, year-end evaluation, or full-length book, do it *your* way. If you innovate for a better any-thing, do it in the way that is right for you. In other words, to borrow a line from Shakespeare, "To thine *own originality* be true." I don't think Shakespeare would mind my changing one word of his fa-mous line.

You must admit, startling as it was, that Luke's sudden decision to eat fifty eggs was *original*. If you saw the film *Cool Hand Luke,* you will easily remember the scene where Luke actu-ally did gulp down fifty hardboiled eggs in an hour, with all his fellow prisoners making bets, either way, on his amazing feat.

No, I'm not suggesting that you learn to do strange feats like this yourself, unless it is your choice. I cite the example of the eggs only to show that even a prisoner in bleak surroundings can come up with *original* ideas—silly though some of them may be. As Luke said, "It was something to do . . . something different." It certainly captured the attention of all those present and entertained them on a boring afternoon.

What Triggers Originality?

A germ of an idea, a fragment, phrase, feeling, emotion, mood, or something you hear (no matter how short or vague) can trigger your originality.

Years ago, I heard about a strange girl who was seen (by a number of people) standing on street corners in the rain trying to hitch a ride. She always was on a corner not far from the cemetery in that area. Some people who told the tale about her said that she was thought to be the *ghost* of some girl who had died tragically and young.

This idea of the girl's ghost standing on corners haunted me. I eventually wrote a short story about the girl. Here is the first paragraph:

> She was getting soaked in the rain, standing there on a corner a few blocks past the Twin Oaks cemetery. As we drove by, I could tell she was a thin wisp of a girl. There was something frantic about the way she was trying to wave a car down. Any car. Without looking at Steve, I turned the car around and headed for her corner.

In my story about the girl, I had two men give her a ride (supposedly when hitchhiking was thought to be safer than it now is). She gives them an address, and the two men drive to Shadow Lane Avenue. But just before they get there, the girl—her ghost, that is—*vanishes* from the back seat of the car. The men knock on the door at the address she gave them. An old woman opens the door, and they tell her about the girl. In tears, the old lady explains that the girl was her daughter who died three years earlier of pneumonia and is buried in the cemetery near the spot where the men saw her. The old woman tells them that it's the third time someone has come to her house with the *same* story.

So listen to the *inner* voice within you. Watch for the signs and signals that may trigger your originality. Be true to yourself. For in reality, *you* are a truly remarkable human being. There's nobody else quite like you. And don't forget it. You're an *original.* Be proud of that fact. And make it count in a world that needs all kinds of original thinking.

In the next chapter, we'll take a look at the importance of rewarding yourself now and then.

Reward Yourself
Now and Then

15

A few months ago, an elderly millionaire killed himself by weighting his body then shooting himself . . . just before jumping into the cold waters of Long Island Sound. He jumped from his own $200,000, three-bedroom yacht.

Obviously, this man was disillusioned and unhappy about something. The fact that he was a millionaire evidently wasn't enough to make up for whatever led him to take his own life.

The point here is that even millionaires can be unhappy and disillusioned. Yet, logically, this man who plunged into Long Island Sound had more than enough money to travel anywhere and buy anything he wished—even a vast array of items to cheer himself up. Then why did he kill himself? Perhaps it was bad health, as one possibility.

There are different kinds of rewards. Most of us are far from being millionaires, but we can still determine to reward ourselves now and then in different ways. You don't have to be a millionaire to bring occasional rewards into your life. No matter who you are, where you live, or what your circumstances may be, there are various ways to brighten up your life.

Reasons for Rewarding Yourself
Now and Then

Along with the fact that it's just good sense to reward yourself occasionally, there are other valid reasons for doing it:

• Commend yourself on a job well done. Let's face it. Your employer, firm, company, office, (or wherever you work) may not recognize or appreciate your good work and continuing contribution. Many employers and companies today fail to reward some of their most valuable workers. It's hard to believe, but it's true.

A talented man from Tennessee gave many of his best years to a large and powerful advertising company. The company kept promising him a key promotion for his excellent work. But the years went by and the long expected promotion to vice-president never came. So after fifteen years, the man called the company's bluff and soon found himself out of a job. Fortunately, because of his experience, he was able to land a new and better position with a company that really appreciates his contributions and shows it.

• Provide yourself with incentives that make life more positive and interesting.

In my navy days, as part of the Sixth Fleet, the top-ranking officers of our carrier were well aware that life can become tedious during long periods of sea duty when you may go for months at a time without even *seeing* land. So the three thousand men aboard our carrier were rewarded with free movies every night, shown on the hangar-bay area of the ship. Other rewards included occasional talent shows, music shows, and the offer of special tours at a very low bargain rate.

I went on a number of the special tours and they were great. On one guided tour of Rome, about fifty of us were taken by bus to the train depot in Genoa, Italy (after our ship had put in at Genoa for a month's stay). We rode a fine train to Rome and had three days there seeing all the sights and historic landmarks. We were lodged in one of the top hotels, with most of our meals included. A guide took us all over Rome on special chartered buses and explained all the history behind the various fountains, churches, the Coliseum, capital buildings area, Vatican City, and the rest.

It was a fabulous three-day tour of Rome, and it even included a glimpse of the Pope (Pius XII), when he waved from a window to an enormous crowd in Vatican square. We were part of that crowd, which had come from all over Europe to be at Vatican City on Christmas Day. The Pope had been ill and could only wave from a window to the large crowd below.

I know you'll be *astounded* at what that three-day guided tour cost me. Incredibly, the entire three-day trip was just $30 per person. It was set up and arranged completely (for the navy) by American Express. A major reason, however, for this great bargain was the year. It was December 1957. Money was worth far more at that time than its spendable value brings today.

• Rewarding yourself now and then can give you a lift, and it also gives you something to look forward to. Life is more than the work routine, chores, duties, and the fulfillment of responsibilities. Most of us need to have something to look forward to . . . something nice we plan to do. Here are just a few of the rewards you can give yourself, depending upon who you are and what your particular situation happens to be:

1. Going to one or more Friday-Saturday night dances
2. Seeing a ball game with a friend
3. Going shopping in your favorite stores or mall
4. Seeing a new quality movie
5. Lunch or dinner with friends
6. Attending a special sports event or concert
7. Treating yourself to a book, a new suit, shoes, hairdo, or whatever
8. A weekend trip to the lake, country, old home town, or resort area
9. Just taking a day off and relaxing . . . or doing whatever you wish

The above list includes just a few of the many possible types of rewards. Some might well wish to include a Coca-Cola, coffee, or tea break, simple walks around the block, an hour in the park, playing golf or tennis, or any number of other items.

Best-selling author Ken Follett has, in recent years, been living on the Riviera. He spent the last three years there and described the weather as "very pleasant" and the restaurants in the area as lovely. After three years, he decided to move back to England. "France will never feel like home and England does."

So living in a different area, whether temporarily or for a period of years, can be still another type of reward. Such rewards naturally cost more in money and time, but they add interest, variety, and knowledge to your life. If you have often longed to spend some time in a certain place or area, why not try to make it a reality? Think of it as a reward you deserve, and be determined to see it happen in your life.

The unforgettable actor Humphrey Bogart frequently rewarded himself by sailing. It was one of his great loves. When he had the time, he took his boat out to sea and found both refreshment and renewal in getting away from it all on the water. He felt strongly that sailing a boat was a mystical experience . . . that being out there with the wind in your face, riding the water with the vast sky above you is both stimulating and highly enjoyable. Behind the cynical characters Bogart often played on the screen, there was a very sincere, deeply humble, and faithful man.

I urge you to find out what little, or considerable rewards work best for you. Then use those rewards. Plan and actually schedule them in your ongoing daily life. They can certainly help you to rise above a sense of disillusionment because they brighten your life and give you something to look forward to. And everyone needs that. Man is not a machine. We all need little rewards in our daily routines and lives. They keep us going.

Zane Grey, the great western author, said it well: "Life is a series of challenges and adjustments to changing situations." Rewarding yourself now and then helps you to meet and handle those challenges and adjustments. And rewarding yourself keeps you walking, living, working, and thinking happy.

Beware of
Modern-Day
Time Killers

16

Another action step you can take to rise above any feelings of disillusionment is to conserve your time and make it count more. This is easier said than done. Modern living has become a mine field, and on any place you step you may be assaulted by an assortment of time killers.

Good intentions aren't enough. At the beginning of each new week, millions of people plan to watch their time more carefully. But try as they do, they often realize by the end of the week how much valuable time has gone down the drain.

Consider the following breakdown of a human lifespan of seventy years:

- Some *one percent* of the time is spent in prebirth development.
- *Three percent* goes to infancy.
- *Fourteen percent* is spent in childhood.
- *Nine percent* is taken for adolescence.
- *Thirty-one percent* is spent in the prime years of life.
- *Twenty-nine percent* is used up in middle age.
- *Thirteen percent* is spent in old age.

By making better use of your time—not wasting this most precious commodity—you can derive a sense of satisfaction and assurance that every day is counting in your life.

Here is a partial list of the modern time killers. Check over each one of them. If you feel that you are presently spending *too much time,* in the indicated ways named on the list, place a check-mark in the appropriate space to the right of each item:

Time Killers	*Too Much Time Being Spent?*	
	YES	NO
1. Watching television	_____	_____
2. Housework	_____	_____
3. Meetings	_____	_____
4. Eating meals	_____	_____
5. Sleeping	_____	_____
6. Club projects	_____	_____
7. Cooking and meal preparation	_____	_____
8. Get-togethers with friends	_____	_____
9. Partying and entertainment	_____	_____
10. Getting the car serviced	_____	_____
11. Shopping	_____	_____
12. Doing your income tax	_____	_____
13. Getting to and from work	_____	_____
14. Listening to problems of others	_____	_____
15. Office paperwork	_____	_____
16. Weekend driving	_____	_____
17. Visiting relatives	_____	_____
18. Playing with the kids	_____	_____
19. Vacations	_____	_____
20. Resolving disagreements	_____	_____
21. Reading	_____	_____
22. Worrying about the budget	_____	_____
23. Talking to neighbors	_____	_____
24. Lawn care	_____	_____
25. Chatting on the telephone	_____	_____

		YES	NO
26.	Going to movies	___	___
27.	Exercise and physical fitness	___	___
28.	Writing letters	___	___
29.	Studying	___	___
30.	Giving speeches	___	___
31.	Playing cards	___	___
32.	Daydreaming	___	___
34.	Playing records	___	___
35.	Keeping a diary	___	___
36.	Going to ball games	___	___
37.	Keeping and checking records	___	___
38.	Listening to the radio	___	___
39.	Arguing with spouse or others	___	___
40.	Hobbies	___	___
41.	Making decisions	___	___
42.	In the shower or bathtub	___	___
43.	Dressing	___	___
44.	Getting advanced degrees	___	___
45.	Voting	___	___
46.	Committee duties	___	___
47.	Finding a new place to live	___	___
48.	Running for office	___	___
49.	Playing a musical instrument	___	___
50.	Remembering	___	___
51.	Planning a wedding	___	___
52.	Smoking	___	___
53.	Feeling disillusioned, depressed, or unhappy	___	___

After placing a checkmark in each appropriate space, add up your total number of YES responses. Place the total number in this space: _____ Now make a list of the items you answered yes to and keep it with you at all times . . . or where you can see and refer to it often. Here is a *master list* of the specific ways in which you feel you are killing too much time. Take each one of these time killers and work on reducing the time you spend on each. When you've cut the time spent on one, move on to the next one on your list. This method really works because it helps you to *focus* on the specific areas where you are spending too much time.

Bruce Catton, the prize-winning author of more than fifteen Civil War books, meant to write his *first* book many years ago. But he kept delaying and putting it off. Finally, on his 49th birthday, Bruce resolved to get a book written before another birthday rolled around. His first book, published before he turned fifty, led him on to such books as *Mister Lincoln's Army, Glory Road,* and *A Stillness at Appomattox.* Maybe Bruce could have turned out additional fine books, if he had gotten started sooner and had not waited until his forty-ninth birthday.

Have you ever noticed how many people under the age of thirty seem to think and act like they've got a long term contract with time? Perhaps it's just part of growing up and becoming a mature person, but a vast amount of time is certainly squandered by the young. Maybe a chief reason for it is that so many young people in their twenties and thirties don't really know who they are yet, what they can do best, the nature of their abilities and talents, or even what they *think* they want to do.

How to Avoid
Life's Time Killers

Here are some proven ways to stand your ground against the daily and weekly assault of a wide host of time killers:

1. Before you climb out of bed in the morning, go over your day in your mind and determine how you can dodge any and all bandits that may threaten to rob you of your time (for that particular day).

2. Go back to the list of time killers presented earlier in this chapter. Make a list of those time killers you answered YES to—

those you indicated are taking too much of your time. *This* time work out a specific plan to reduce the particular item. Get a pocket notebook or three-ring binder and record any and all ideas, pointers you come across, suggestions from friends and associates, things you read, and information from any source you believe will help you . . . in that particular area.

3. Place a large sign, or one written in red letters, where you can see it day and night. Have one in your home and another at the place where you work. Here are the words of the sign: "Do not squander time, for that is the stuff life is made of."

Believe me. Just seeing this sign (in red letters) several times a day will help you to be much more aware of anything and everything that is swallowing up your time.

A complete overhaul of the way you now spend much of your time may be needed. But I assure you that it is quite possible to get *far more* out of each twenty-four-hour period and the rest of the week as well.

Beware of the time killers named in this chapter. You may well know of others you can add to the list. Refer back to this chapter and follow the suggestions given in it. You'll be surprised at how much more you can accomplish, even in several months or less, by watching your time more carefully.

Like the great old song title says so well, "It's funny how the time slips away." In reality, it's your life slipping away. So spend the time you have wisely and carefully. It's a priceless treasure!

Find a Cause You Can Believe in

17

Still another practical way to wipe out a sense of disillusionment is to forget it by joining and working for a cause you believe in strongly. You will find a number of worthy causes suggested in this chapter.

The beauty of getting interested in a cause is that it absorbs you, keeps you busy, and provides you with a sense of real satisfaction. Go to work for a cause and you'll feel like you're making your life and time count more.

In recent years, the American public has clamored for a return to education basics. Citizens from all walks of life have joined forces to support the cause of focusing new and stronger attention on reading, writing, and math in schools across the country.

There Are All Kinds of Causes

Some types of causes are more interesting, time consuming, and involved than others. Here are some of the various kinds of causes:

1. *Seminar programs* on various concerns, such as health and fitness. Discussions are held in these programs on the handling of stress, lack of exercise, poor nutrition, smoking, and the excessive use of alcohol.

2. *Personal causes* include fund-raising drives of all types. Entertainer Danny Thomas, for example, has dedicated himself completely to seeing that St. Jude Hospital in Memphis, Tennessee will have enough money to keep operating for many years to come.

Another example is a man who lives in the historic Black Hills area of South Dakota. His name is Korczak Ziolkowski, and he has spent many years carving a vision in stone on a mountain there in the Black Hills. His vision is a carved memorial to the Indian chief, Crazy Horse.

A Reader's Digest book on the seven wonders of the modern world includes the Crazy Horse carving with this heading: "Made in America on a scale that dwarfs the dreams of the ancients." A caption under the picture of the sculpture reads: "Chief Crazy Horse gallops into battle." The amazing carving, near Custer, South Dakota, will stand 561 feet high and 641 feet long. Seven-and-a-half million tons of granite will have been moved in the process.

Korczak had never heard of Crazy Horse before becoming interested in his project. "I didn't know any Indians. But Standing Bear and I walked these hills and looked for a place for the memorial. I thought about a one hundred-foot statue at first, but it grew and grew."

The mountain Korczak carved on came first. As he puts it, "I told my wife years ago that the mountain came first, then the children, then her." His wife, Ruth, has talked to the governor and others, written letters, and helped in many other ways on the project.

When he started work on the memorial, Korczak carried lumber on his back. It was for a 740 step stairway up the mountain so he could get to work. He then had to carry a drill, hammer, chisel, and dynamite up there.

As he made progress on the carving, celebrities, writers, and many curious people came to visit. "Walter Brennan got to be a good friend," recalled Korczak. Twice he even turned down a $10 million offer from the government. The reason was because Korczak feels "it can't be a government project."

3. *Local, civic, and national causes* can vary from support asked by the Shriners . . . to scout groups, research money to find cures for human diseases, to arts programs sponsored by large associations.

Worthy National Causes

Here are a number of respected national causes well worth your consideration. Many of them have local or regional branch offices. You can write to them and ask how you can help. In addition to financial contributions to those of your choice, you may be able to help in other ways. Most of them will be happy to send you some information about their work. The addresses given are subject to change:

Alcoholics Anonymous (1935)
Box 459
New York, New York 10017

Allied Youth (1936)
933 North Kenmore Street
Arlington, Virginia 22201

American Aging Association (1970)
University of Nebraska Medical Center
Omaha, Nebraska 68105

American Bible Society (1816)
1865 Broadway
New York, New York 10023

American Cancer Society (1913)
219 East 42nd Street
New York, New York 10017

American Diabetes Association (1940)
One West 48th Street
New York, New York 10020

American Heart Association (1924)
44 East 23rd Street
New York, New York 10010

American Library Association (1876)
50 East Huron Street
Chicago, Illinois 60611

American Lung Association (1904)
1740 Broadway
New York, New York 10019

American Public Health Association (1972)
1015 18th Street, Southwest
Washington, D.C. 20036

Arthritis Foundation (1948)
475 Riverside Drive
New York, New York 10027

Big Brothers/Big Sisters of America (1977)
220 Suburban Station Building
Philadelphia, Pennsylvania 19103

Boy's Clubs of America (1860)
771 First Avenue
New York, New York 10017

Boy Scouts of America (1910)
North Brunswick, New Jersey 08902

Campfire Girls (1910)
4601 Madison Avenue
Kansas City, Missouri 64112

CARE (Cooperative for American Relief Everywhere) (1945)
660 First Avenue
New York, New York 10016

Childbirth Without Pain Leagues (1964)
P.O. Box 233
Dana Point, California 92629

Child Welfare League of America (1920)
67 Irving Place
New York, New York 10003

Council for a Livable World (1962)
100 Maryland Avenue, Northeast
Washington, D.C. 20002

Family Service Association of America (1911)
44 East 23rd Street
New York, New York 10010

Girl's Clubs of America (1945)
133 East 62nd Street
New York, New York 10021

International Association for Pollution Control (1970)
1625 Eye Street, Northwest
Washington, D.C. 20006

March of Dimes (1938)
1275 Mamaroneck Avenue
White Plains, New York 10605

National Association for Creative Children and Adults (1974)
8080 Springvalley Drive
Cincinnati, Ohio 45236

National Association for Retarded Citizens (1950)
2709 Avenue E East
East Arlington, Texas 76011

National Association of the Physically Handicapped (1958)
6473 Grandville
Detroit, Michigan 48228

National Audubon Society
850 Third Avenue
New York, New York 10022

National Council of Crime and Delinquency (1907)
411 Hackensack Avenue
Hackensack, New Jersey 07601

National Easter Seal Society for Crippled Children & Adults
2023 West Ogden Avenue
Chicago, Illinois 60612

National Federation of the Blind (1940)
218 Randolph Hotel
Des Moines, Iowa 50309

National Fire Protection Association (1896)
470 Atlantic Avenue
Boston, Massachusetts 02210

National Multiple Sclerosis Society (1946)
257 Park Avenue South
New York, New York 10010

National Safety Council (1913)
425 North Michigan Avenue
Chicago, Illinois 60611

National Wildlife Federation (1936)
Washington, D.C. 20036

Parents Without Partners (1957)
7910 Woodmont Avenue
Washington, D.C. 20014

Parkinson's Disease Foundation (1957)
640 West 168th Street
New York, New York 10032

Radio Free Europe (1949)
2 Park Avenue
New York, New York 10016

Research to Prevent Blindness (1960)
598 Madison Avenue
New York, New York 10022

Salvation Army (1880)
120 West 14th Street
New York, New York 10011

Space Exploration Establishment (1977)
3775 Hambletonian Drive
Florissant, Missouri 63033

Travelers Aid-International Social Service of America (1972)
345 East 46th Street
New York, New York 10017

United Cerebral Palsy Association (1948)
66 East 34th Street
New York, New York 10016

Questions
and Answers
on Disillusionment

18

The following questions are some of the most frequently asked about disillusionment:

Why do I feel melancholy so often?

Some degree of this feeling is caused by the uncertain times we live in today. It's natural to feel like this some of the time. If it persists, however, your condition could be chronic, calling for a visit to your doctor's office.

For some years now, nothing has gone the way I wanted it to in my life. How can I handle this disappointment?

One way is to become a realist. When we're in high school, many of us fantasize and think that everything will be better after we've graduated and have gone on to college. Then, in college, we think we'll be happier if we can just get that first good job. After landing it, we think the next answer is the right house in the sub-urbs, or job promotion, or whatever.

In other words, we delude ourselves into believing that all will be to our liking once we move ahead one more notch on the horizon. Nothing seems as good when we get there as we thought it was going to be. There's a danger here, obviously, of living too much in the future and wishing your life away.

120

Can disillusionment be caused by wanting something out of reach?

Yes. If one sets his or her heart on getting or achieving a certain thing and it doesn't materialize, disillusionment can be the result. Some people become disillusioned when the feeling of being satisfied eludes them. Emerson warned of three specific wants: "There are three wants which can never be satisfied: that of the rich, who wants something more; that of the sick, who wants something different; and that of the traveler, who says, 'anywhere but here.'

Isn't disillusionment just another word for disappointment?

Many people certainly view it this way. If you go after big chunks of happiness, you will probably be disappointed. A strong case can be made for seeking the little bits and pieces of happiness. They can often add up to a good-sized chunk anyway. "Happiness is having had a good night's sleep and not being hurt by new shoes," said Theodor Fontane, the German novelist and poet.

Can you suggest some remedies for disillusionment?

Some people report good results from giving their interest to others. Millions want fame and fortune, and if they don't attain them, they find little joy in life. It's the big time or bust for such people. They get so starry-eyed that they miss the stardust all around them. They concentrate too much on what they're going to get, rather than on giving. Giving of your talents, abilities, time, and interest to others can be a tonic for feelings of disillusionment.

Why do so many people here and overseas experience depression and the blues?

There is some truth in the old cliché that "you have to take the bitter with the sweet." There seems to be a corresponding letdown as the direct opposite of feeling optimistic and happy. You can take definite comfort in knowing that practically everyone has gone through the horror of the blues. The great British leader Winston Churchill had a good name for the blues or depression. He summed them up as "the black dog."

121

After being shot at on a daily basis in Viet Nam and coming close to death several times, I found, on my return home, that everything in civilian life seemed completely trivial and without meaning. I still get this overwhelming feeling at times. Will it ever leave me for good?

I believe it will, even if it continues to recede from your life slowly. With the continued passing of time, you should be much better. Try to spend your time in work you find interesting and do fun things in your spare time. Refer to chapter twelve in this book for guidelines on getting into work you can like or love.

Reading the newspaper is the most disillusioning experience of my daily routine, but I go on doing it, even though I always feel depressed and letdown afterward. Do you have any suggestions?

If you can manage to kick the newspaper habit, you might try depending on television news mainly, but it often has the same effect. Mark Twain once said that the happiest period in his entire life was the seven years he did not pick up a newspaper.

I'm unemployed and recently responded to an ad for a job. When I called the company on the telephone, I was told that somebody already known by the company had the job locked up. My question, then, is why they run the ad and waste my time and that of others who will answer it?

I think it boils down to integrity. Some companies and executives lack integrity. I've heard rumors for years that some employment agencies run blind ads for jobs that don't even exist. The ads are meant to lure people looking for jobs into their offices and to get applications completed on them.

After working my way through college, I quickly discovered that a degree means little. Do you think that a college education will ever have the value it once did?

It still does have value in the sense that it teaches one to think and provides a base of knowledge about a variety of academic disciplines. But many employers and companies are evidently placing more emphasis now on personal initiative. Still, a great many potential employers won't even talk to an applicant who doesn't have a college degree. In other words, a degree is usually the minimum, square-one requirement. Many today think of degrees as basic union cards.

What has disillusioned me the most, as a middle-aged person, is to realize that I can count my real friends on the fingers of one hand. Whatever happened to friendship?

People change over the years. They often forget old friends or just don't have the time for them they once did. Keep in mind, however, that making a living and trying to get ahead, as so many millions are doing, doesn't leave as much time as it once did to maintain friendships.

So many of my friends and loved ones are gone now that I find life empty. Everything seems to have gone for nothing. Will I get over this?

The world can indeed seem like a strange place when one's loved ones and close friends are no longer around. I would encourage you to focus on the beautiful things in life that you still have . . . including your health, hobbies, the joy of travel, all the wonderful books and magazines available to you, good music, and a vast array of other good things about living. And don't forget that you can certainly make new friends.

Use the Proverbs as a Guide for Living

19

My grandmother was a strong and enthusiastic believer in centering your life around the wisdom of the basic proverbs. I grew up hearing her quote various proverbs daily, and they really helped her to be a happier and more successful person. My family eventually nicknamed my grandmother "the Proverb Lady" because of her great fondness for these words of wisdom.

I know that many of these proverbs can be of help to you in rising above any feelings of disillusionment. Such proverbs were, of course, taken more seriously in the early decades of this century. Today, in more modern times, they are often laughed at and thought to be amusing. But they are well worth keeping in mind and using in your life. And you may well decide to center your life on these proverbs. Here are some of the best known ones:

1. *Strike while the iron is hot.* This one obviously refers to opportunity. In other words, you must do what you can to advance yourself . . . and try to do it at the *right* time. Timing is of utmost importance. Many let four-star opportunities go by. They don't strike while the iron is hot. An opportunity seized at the right moment can change your life.

2. *Laugh, and the world laughs with you.* Your basic attitude is the important thing here. Answer the following questions:

126

A. Can you see things in the proper perspective?

B. Do you have the ability to laugh at yourself?

C. Does humor have an important place in your life and routine?

By striving to see the humor in any number of life's situations, you can definitely grow as a person and also snap back from the effects of disillusionment. Robert Benchley, the famed author and beloved humorist, had the right spirit. He once remarked on the time needed to develop writing ability: "It took me fifteen years to discover I had no talent for writing, but I couldn't give it up because by that time I was too famous."

3. *Who loses honor can lose nothing else.* One of the most interesting things about Japan is the country's remarkably high sense of honor. In view of the frequently reported scandals and corruption in high places in America, even involving members of Congress via Abscam, it would seem that honor is not what it used to be.

Honor is a great ideal to hold, cherish, and practice. A tragedy of today is the fact that many in our nation have lost faith, trust, and confidence in either political party. Countless millions refuse to cast their votes, replying only that "there isn't a dime's worth of difference between the two major political parties."

4. *Actions speak louder than words.* This proverb has been heard and read so often that it has practically become a cliché. It is certainly true that the best way to judge someone is by his or her actions and not simply by what is said. Sit in on courtroom decisions made every working day, and you'll quickly realize that most judges must render their decisions based on the *actions* of those before the bench. They may promise the judge never to repeat the offense again, but their records speak for themselves. If they repeatedly break the law, they must bear the penalty for their actions. Likewise, marriage vows are lovely to hear, but just how important they really are to the bride and groom remains to be seen in the future years of their marriage.

5. *They are never alone that are accompanied with noble thoughts.* To a very large degree, you live within your thoughts. It seems evident that if your thoughts are noble and courageous ones, you won't be dragged down into the mud of despair, disillusionment, and depression.

Never forget that *thoughts are things.* By dwelling on thoughts of defeat, hopelessness, and despair, you are actually increasing the combined forces of such negative thoughts. And this in turn will give them more power to rule and control you. Never let them gain control in your mind and life, and you'll win the battle against disillusionment. In fact, you will have already won it.

6. *Let not the sun go down upon your wrath.* Anger is a sheer waste of human energy. It's a proven fact now that anger, if strong enough, can make the angry person ill. Anger is also responsible for the following:

- Anger can ruin your day or week.
- Anger doesn't solve anything.
- Anger can ruin your lunch or dinner and bring on indigestion.
- Anger often works like a boomerang; it comes back to you.
- Anger is vivid proof that a person has little or no self-control.

7. *All would live long, but none would be old.* When I was a teenager, I well remember thinking that anyone over forty was ancient. But now that I'm over forty myself, I've changed my thinking entirely. Realizing now how quickly the years go, I feel strongly that *any age under one hundred is young.*

Consider also the following truths about growing older, which is something none of us can help doing:

- Growing older beats the alternative.
- If and when birthdays depress you, think of these words by Robert Browning: "Come grow old with me, the best of life is yet to be."
- Growing older brings compensations with it including increased wisdom, a keener understanding, more appreciation for the many good things in life, and gratitude for having been a part of it all. Bing Crosby once summed up the Christmas season in this way: "Christmas is a time for being thankful that you could come this far."

8. *Patience opens all doors.* One of the best places to learn the art of patience is in military service. You rush one place only to stand in line. Anyone who has ever been in any branch of the military will know what I mean. I was honorably discharged from the navy at Norfolk, Virginia, after serving on active duty and complet-

ing my military obligation. The red tape involved in getting pro-
cessed out of the service was unbelievable. It took almost four
weeks of living in a barracks on the base before all the paperwork
could be completed for about seventy-five of us being discharged
at the same time. Some of us would meet daily and wonder just
how much longer it was going to take before we would be civilians
again. Going into the navy, by contrast, was much much faster and
practically as smooth as silk, to use an old cliché.

Patience is difficult for many to develop, but it does pay
dividends. With patience, a lot of things may look, and truly are,
much more possible. Look at the patience needed to find a new
job. At this writing, several million unemployed Americans have
reportedly given up on finding a position. They are termed the
"discouraged unemployed." In other words, these people have
simply run out of patience.

Other worthy and memorable proverbs include the following:

9. *Hitch your wagon to a star.*
10. *Beauty is a fading flower.*
11. *There is no education like adversity.*
12. *Better to be alone than in bad company.*
13. *Everyone excels in something in which another fails.*
14. *The fool hath said in his heart, there is no God.*
15. *Birds of a feather flock together.*
16. *There is nothing permanent except change.*
17. *Take things as they come.*
18. *The test of courage is to bear defeat without losing heart.*
19. *He loves his country best who strives to make it best.*
20. *A fool and his money are soon parted.*

Chase
Some Rainbows

20

A strange thing happened to me on my fortieth birthday. I had a mental flashback to my high school days. For ten minutes or so, I was once again in the twelfth grade thinking about which college I might best like to attend the following year and trying to decide what field of work interested me the most.

It seems like only yesterday that I was concerned with high school and college dances, parties, English themes, football games, algebra tests, school plays, and my daily paper route. In truth it was only yesterday. Inside I still don't feel a day over eighteen, even though my receding hairline, gray temples, and expanding waistline tell a different story.

Looking back on those happy high school and college days made me realize that something I feel is quite valid: You've got to try your wings, ideally when you're young. But no matter what your age, you need to chase some rainbows.

The Dreams of Youth . . .
at All Ages

You no doubt have a dream right now—something you would like to achieve, accomplish, or become more than anything else in the world. But perhaps you feel the odds are against you, or you can't believe you could really go that particular route at this time in your life.

What about it? Have you got one or more dreams or strong interests? Have you acted on one or more of them? Have you gone after it with all the gusto and interest of your youth? If not, I strongly urge you to do so.

Perhaps you feel that you'll get around later to trying your wings at your special dream. You might do so, and then again you may find yourself caught up in circumstances and the busy events of your life. After school and college comes a probable stint in the military (at least for many men and some women), a first job, and maybe marriage. One day you wake up and you're twenty-five, although these early years often seem like they are dragging by.

In other words, once your school or college days are over, you lose track of old friends, perhaps move to another city or section of the country, marry, and continue to grow in your job, career, or profession. Suddenly it's birthday time again, and it dawns on you that you've hit the big thirty.

About this time you ask yourself some questions, if only in your mind:

1. What happened to that dream (or dreams) I had years ago?
2. Why didn't I go after some of the things I really thought I'd like to at least try—despite the odds being against my getting to do them?
3. Do I really like the way things are shaping up for me at this point in my life?

You're probably going to remember the rainbows you once had and wonder why you didn't pursue them more actively, before you got so busy and involved with the passing years.

The good news at this point in your life, regardless of your age, is that you still have time to go after those rainbows. After all, thirty is still a "young" age, isn't it? So is thirty-five. So is forty-five.

Here is where I want to warn you. Once you pass the big thirty, time moves like a toboggan. Many remember how the years from twenty to thirty seemed to go by at a slow to medium rate of speed. Believe me, time measured in months and years sprouts wings and flies after thirty. In fact, each decade beyond thirty goes twice as fast as the preceding one. This period of time may be your last real chance to follow that dream in your heart or try your wings along some pathway of interest to you.

I knew myself, for example, back in my junior year of college, that one of the rainbows I wanted to try was professional acting. I realized that if I didn't try my wings at it during my youthful twenties, I might never get another real chance. So I acted on this idea by auditioning for a job as a summer stock actor. Only one other fellow from my university tried out, although many students from a variety of colleges auditioned for roles. I think the other students from my university were either scared at the prospect of performing on stage, or were simply booked up with other plans for the summer.

I was nervous when I auditioned, but I did my best. The same was true for my fellow student. Fortunately, both of us were able to speak loud, and this was a big plus in our favor. We would be signing as professional actors for the summer (1955) in "Unto These Hills," the outdoor dramatic pageant production located in the heart of the Smoky Mountains near Cherokee, North Carolina. The theater was built on the side of one mountain and seated over three thousand people. The director wanted actors who could project their speaking voices loud enough to be heard by those sitting in the top last row of the theater. It was one of the best summers of my life, and I still remember the pleasure of hearing that I had been offered the acting job for the summer.

Rainbow Number Two

A second rainbow I went after took place during my two years in the navy. As a yeoman aboard the U.S.S. *Roosevelt,* a carrier, I typed naval correspondence between our ship and Washington. But in my free time at night and on liberty during weekends, I was busy writing songs. I had caught the songwriting bug sometime before starting my naval service.

I got some results with my songs, despite my young age (twenty-two). One of my songs won a national magazine contest. I stuck with it and went on to win two national awards for songs, to hear a number of my songs performed in nightclubs, and to see others recorded nationally. Most of the one thousand songs I wrote during my twenties were not up to par, but about fifteen of them were very strong numbers. Another rainbow of mine was reached during those years, when I became a full member of ASCAP, the American Society of Composers, Authors, and Publishers.

Now here is an important point. My songs were not huge hits. I never got a big hit song, but I had the *enormous* satisfaction of going after something I had always wanted to do from my teen years on—to create new songs and hear them performed and recorded.

So the rainbow I chased brought me a lot of fulfillment. But I know that if I had waited until my thirties or forties, I wouldn't have tried to write even one song. Songwriting was something I *had* to pursue. And I've always been glad that I did. The moment's enthusiasm somehow led me to try my hand at songwriting . . . no matter what.

Chasing Rainbows Can Lead to a Lifetime Career

Songwriting did not turn out to be my life work, but it did for others who also were willing to chase and *catch* that rainbow.

In 1930 at a Friday night basketball game and dance at Woodmere Academy on Long Island, Johnny Loeb, a cousin of the murdered Bobbie Franks (the victim of the infamous Leopold-Loeb case), asked his friend, Paul Webster, if he had ever written a song. Surprised at the question, Webster said that he hadn't and knew nothing about songwriting. But the question got the two of them thinking.

After the dance that night, on a used piano above the school gym, Webster and Loeb wrote a song. It was a waltz called "Masquerade." Webster has often thought back on that eventful night: "The light had been shut off, so we used a cigarette lighter while creating and writing the song."

This strange beginning was Webster's first attempt at songwriting, but it changed his life. "I might never have started writing if my friend Loeb hadn't asked me that question.

Webster could have dropped it the next few weeks and months. He didn't. He tried his wings. He chased the rainbow. Every publisher in New York turned down "Masquerade." Still convinced the song had something, Webster took a train to Chicago to see Paul Whiteman at the Edgewater Beach Hotel. It took three nights of waiting before he finally got a chance to talk Whiteman into listening to "Masquerade."

Whiteman liked the song and agreed to introduce it the following month in New York. A symphonic arrangement was done, and the song was published by a leading New York publisher (Leo Feist). "Masquerade" earned $12,000 for each of its two creators. That was a lot of money in 1930. Above all, this rainbow pursued by Webster turned out to be his life work. Webster went on to write most of the top songs for Shirley Temple during the 1930s and to win no less than three Academy Awards during the years of his career for such unforgettable songs as "Secret Love," "Love Is a Many-Splendored Thing," and "The Shadow of Your Smile."

So listen to the interests of your mind, spirit, and heart. When a rainbow beckons, go after it at least for awhile and see what happens. You find yourself by trying your wings, and soaring *above* disillusionment. The best time to do it, to chase those rainbows, is now.

Appendixes

A Self-Scoring Test
on Coping with Disillusionment

Answer the following questions with either a YES or NO. Then follow the directions after the test for figuring your score and evaluating it. I suggest that you take this test *again* in six months and then compare your two scores. Here are the questions:

		YES	NO
1.	Are you *now* doing something about any feelings of disillusionment?	_____	_____
2.	Have you discovered what the causes are for your disillusionment?	_____	_____
3.	Do you understand how swiftly the months and years of your life are going by?	_____	_____
4.	Do you believe that a temporary sense of disillusionment can later influence a person to appreciate life more?	_____	_____
5.	Do you really make the most of every opportunity that comes your way?	_____	_____
6.	Do you rely on your inner resources to help you rise above feelings of disillusionment?	_____	_____

	YES	NO

7. Do you feel that it's better to light a small candle of hope and faith . . . than to curse the darkness? _____ _____

8. Have you ever tried to *think* your way out of disillusionment by focusing on the many good and positive things about your life? _____ _____

9. Do you believe that most people are disillusioned about something at one time or another in their lives? _____ _____

10. Do you agree with the statement that, to a large extent, you have to make *your own* happiness? _____ _____

Directions for Scoring Your Test

Give yourself ten points for each YES answer and zero for each NO answer. Add up your score and place the total in this space: _____

EVALUATION OF YOUR TEST SCORE

Score	*Meaning*
90 to 100	You are doing EXCELLENT in handling a sense of disillusionment.
80 to 90	The way you are coping with feelings of disillusionment rates three stars.
70 to 80	All in all, you are facing disillusionment in a fair, or average, way. Strive to upgrade this score to a higher one.
60 to 70	You're on a conditional margin here between average and defeat. Try to improve.
50 to 60	Disillusionment apparently has you down for the count. You're out of the ball park with this score.

Checklist for Achieving a Greater Sense of Satisfaction

1. Try to touch the lives of others in a good, helpful, or inspiring way.
2. Strive to make a lasting contribution with your time, abilities, talents, and overall life in general.

3. Tune up and develop your imagination. Always have at least three imaginative projects in the works.

4. Treasure the invaluable gift of each new day and try to make your time count more.

5. Don't go to bed at night until you *know* what your major priorities and objectives are for the next day.

6. Be a consistently loyal friend.

7. Be more willing to take chances and to risk possible failure. Every day is a gamble in a number of ways.

8. Remember that *everyone* is disillusioned at various times in their lives. It's what you do about it that is important.

9. Realize that running away from reality never solves anything. The problem is usually still there when you get back.

10. Resolve and be determined to make your own happiness.

11. Go back to school. There are so many fascinating things to discover. Learning can become a joy in itself.

12. Keep your mind and spirit focused on life's lovely intangibles including goodness, beauty, honor, truth, and love.

13. Strive to develop your inner resources including extra strength, the ability to bounce back from what life throws at you, the realization that aloneness doesn't have to mean loneliness, hope for the future, the ability to entertain yourself, and self-control.

14. Visit occasionally in the mountains. Spending time in the mountains, whether the Smokies or the Rockies, can be uplifting and very satisfying. A walk along a beach can be equally therapeutic.

15. Keep in mind that big goals take longer to achieve. Don't flog yourself for not attaining them in too short a time period.

16. Always know that you're a multimillionaire if you have good health. Never take your health for granted.

17. Don't underestimate your potential by failing to realize the power of your mind.

18. Cherish your integrity. It is worth more than rubies and gold. By integrity I mean acting responsibly and doing what you *say* you are going to do.

19. Strive to be a more confident person and to express confidence in others. As an example, John Wayne was a tall timber of confidence. As Bob Hope once said, "It gave us all a real belt to see him each time."

20. Remember the words of General George S. Patton: "It doesn't matter whether you win or lose, as long as you do your damnedest."

21. Recognize that the universe is still in God's hands. He is going to have the last word. He, alone, controls the end of history.

22. Attend a retreat center (for prayer and contemplation) a few times a year. This can be a real help to you.

23. When you pray, ask for . . . and *expect* . . . direction and guidance for your future.

24. Devise and follow specific exercises meant to increase your imagination. Turn back to page 51 and make a real effort to complete the *three* exercise assignments listed there. When you have finished them, plan and follow through on new exercises.

25. Be an inspiring person. There are people in your life who look up to you and can learn from your example.

26. If and when you believe you would be happier in another line of work, follow through on this idea. Investigate the opportunities in other fields and talk to some people. Take the short test on pages 82–83 in this book. "Happy is the man who has found his true work." "Happy is the woman who knows which work field she can love and makes her way in it."

27. Each and every time you feel the odds are stacked against you, turn at once to page 86 in this book and read over the material headed "Winning Against the Odds."

28. Recognize the fact that wealth with all the trimmings is no guarantee of happiness. Princess Grace had the ultimate in material things, but she wasn't as happy as a great many people thought.

29. Throw a surprise party on occasion for someone in your life.

30. Be yourself. You're an original. There is nobody else just like you.

31. Encourage your spark of originality. Do this by being receptive to new innovations, ideas, methods, systems, or whatever. Try something new and daring.

32. Take time to reward yourself now and then for a job well done, as an incentive, or simply to give yourself a lift.

33. Find a cause you can believe in and then sign up, support the organization, attend any meetings, read the literature, and generally climb aboard the bandwagon. For a list of worthy causes, turn to pages 114–117.

34. Test out the proverbs as a guide for living and see if you don't realize a greater sense of satisfaction. Twenty of these proverbs are presented in chapter nineteen.

Suggested Reading

BACH, MARCUS, *The Wonderful Magic of Living.* New York: Doubleday, 1968.

BRANDE, DOROTHEA THOMPSON, *Wake Up and Live.* New York: Cornerstone Library, 1971.

BROTHERS, JOYCE, *How to Get Whatever You Want Out of Life.* New York: Simon and Schuster, 1978.

KORDA, MICHAEL, *Power! How to Get It, How to Use It.* New York: Random House, 1975.

KORDA, MICHAEL, *Success.* New York: Random House, 1977.

LITVAK, STUART, *Use Your Head: How to Develop the Other 80% of Your Brain.* Englewood Cliffs, New Jersey: Prentice-Hall, Inc., 1982.

PEALE, NORMAN VINCENT, *The Power of Positive Thinking.* Englewood Cliffs, New Jersey: Prentice-Hall, Inc., 1952.

SLAGLE, KATE WALSH, *Live with Loss.* Englewood Cliffs, New Jersey: Prentice-Hall, Inc., 1982.

WILBUR, L. PERRY, *The Fast Track to Success.* Englewood Cliffs, New Jersey: Prentice-Hall, Inc., 1982.

WILBUR, L. PERRY, *How to Enjoy Yourself: The Antidote Book for Unhappiness and Depression.* Englewood Cliffs, New Jersey: Prentice-Hall, Inc., 1982.

WILBUR L. PERRY, *Money in Your Mailbox.* Reston, Virginia: Reston Publishing, 1979.

Index